Target
Get back on track

GRADE **9**

Edexcel GCSE (9–1)
English Language
Reading

T0346307

David Grant

PEARSON

Published by Pearson Education Limited, 80 Strand, London, WC2R ORL.

www.pearsonschoolsandfecolleges.co.uk

Text © Pearson Education Limited 2017
Produced and typeset by Tech-Set Ltd, Gateshead

The right of David Grant to be identified as author of this work has been asserted by him in accordance with the Copyright, Designs and Patents Act 1988.

First published 2017

20 19
10 9 8 7 6 5 4 3

British Library Cataloguing in Publication Data
A catalogue record for this book is available from the British Library

ISBN 978 0435 18327 1

Printed in Slovakia by Neografia

We are grateful to the following for permission to reproduce copyright material:

Text
Extract on page 10 Excerpts from THIS BOY'S LIFE copyright © 1989 by Tobias Wolff. Used by permission of Grove/Atlantic, Inc. Any third party use of this material, outside of this publication, is prohibited and 'This Boy's Life' by Tobias Wolff. Grove Press, 2000. International Creative Management, Partners. As agents for Owner. Used by Permission. All rights reserved.; **Article on page 26** from Social media is making us depressed: let's learn to turn it off; Social media is addictive, and like all drugs, it's doing us more harm than good; Janet Street-Porter @The_Real_JSP Friday 8 April 2016. The Independent.; **Extract on page page 58** From *H is for Hawk* by Helen Macdonald Published by Jonathan Cape Reprinted by permission of The Random House Group Limited and Excerpt from H IS FOR HAWK by Helen Macdonald copyright © 2014 by Helen Macdonald. Used by permission of Grove/Atlantic, Inc. Any third party use of this material, outside of this publication, is prohibited.; **Extract on page 58** from *All Things Wise and Wonderful*, 1ed, Pan Macmillan (James Herriot) Used with permission by David Higham Associates Ltd.; **Article on page 73** from Just back: a window on Warsaw, *The Telegraph* 03/04/2009 (Lynda Bailey), Telegraph Media Group Ltd 2016.; **Extract on page 74** from *English Journey*, Special 75th Anniversary Edition, Great Northern Books Ltd (J. B. Priestley 2009), United Agents on behalf of The Estate of J.B. Priestley

Contents

1 Tackling an unseen text
Get started — 1
1 How do I question the text before and while reading it? — 3
2 How do I question the text after reading it? — 4
3 How do I consider different readings of the text? — 5
Get back on track — 6

2 Analysing a text
Get started — 9
1 How do I choose what to analyse? — 11
2 How do I structure my analysis? — 12
3 How do I develop my analysis? — 13
Get back on track — 14

3 Commenting on language
Get started — 17
1 How do I focus my comments on language? — 19
2 How do I develop my comments on language? — 20
3 How do I comment on tone? — 21
Get back on track — 22

4 Commenting on structure
Get started — 25
1 How do I comment on whole text structure? — 27
2 How do I identify the impact that sentence stucture can have? — 28
3 How do I comment on the writer's use of structure? — 29
Get back on track — 30

5 Commenting on language and structure
Get started — 33
1 How do I choose the right evidence from the text? — 35

2 How do I build a comment on language and structure? — 36
3 How do I comment on patterns of language and structure? — 37
Get back on track — 38

6 Evaluating texts
Get started — 41
1 What makes a text successful? — 43
2 Do I analyse or evaluate? — 44
3 How do I structure an evaluation? — 46
Get back on track — 46

7 Synthesising and comparing
Get started — 49
1 How do I synthesise key points? — 51
2 How do I compare synthesised points? — 52
3 How do I structure my comparison? — 53
Get back on track — 54

8 Comparing ideas and perspectives
Get started — 57
1 How do I identify relevant ideas and perspectives? — 59
2 How do I compare ideas and perspectives? — 60
3 How do I develop my comparison? — 61
Get back on track — 62

9 Expressing your ideas clearly and precisely
Get started — 65
1 How do I express my ideas concisely? — 67
2 How do I express my ideas precisely? — 68
3 How do I express my ideas clearly? — 69
Get back on track — 70

More practice texts — 73
Answers — 76

 This workbook has been developed using the Pearson Progression Map and Scale for English.

To find out more about the Progression Scale for English and to see how it relates to indicative GCSE 9–1 grades go to www.pearsonschools.co.uk/ProgressionServices

Helping you to formulate grade predictions, apply interventions and track progress.

Any reference to indicative grades in the Pearson Target Workbooks and Pearson Progression Services is not to be used as an accurate indicator of how a student will be awarded a grade for their GCSE exams.

You have told us that mapping the Steps from the Pearson Progression Maps to indicative grades will make it simpler for you to accumulate the evidence to formulate your own grade predictions, apply any interventions and track student progress. We're really excited about this work and its potential for helping teachers and students. It is, however, important to understand that this mapping is for guidance only to support teachers' own predictions of progress and is not an accurate predictor of grades.

Our Pearson Progression Scale is criterion referenced. If a student can perform a task or demonstrate a skill, we say they are working at a certain Step according to the criteria. Teachers can mark assessments and issue results with reference to these criteria which do not depend on the wider cohort in any given year. For GCSE exams however, all Awarding Organisations set the grade boundaries with reference to the strength of the cohort in any given year. For more information about how this works please visit: https://qualifications.pearson.com/en/support/support-topics/results-certification/understanding-marks-and-grades.html/Teacher

The activities in this workbook have been developed to support students in attaining the 10th, 11th and 12th Steps in the Progression Scale, focusing on those barriers to progression identified in the Pearson Progression Scale.

10th Step	11th Step	12th Step
Evaluates comprehension and **reading skills** during and after reading. Summarises, synthesises and makes a range of perceptive connections between a text's **key points**. Frequently considers patterns of **inference**. Increasingly analytical **critical responses** explore the implications and intention of the writer's **whole text** and **language** choices.	Evaluates comprehension and **reading skills**, consistently questioning the text. Summarises, synthesises and connects **key points**, and may consider alternative interpretations. Consistently considers patterns of **inference**. Perceptive, evaluative **critical responses** explore a range of implications in the writer's **whole text** and **language** choices.	Monitoring and evaluation of **reading skills** are largely automatic. Summarises, synthesises and connects **key points**, reaching astute conclusions. Considers and compares layers of **inference**. Independent **critical responses**, which may explore multiple readings, are supported with confident and perceptive analysis of the writer's **whole text** and **language** choices.

Unit title and **skills boost**	Pearson Progression Scale: Barriers (difficulties students may encounter when working towards this step)	Assessment Objectives	Texts used and paper covered
Unit 1 Tackling an unseen text **Skills boost 1** How do I question the text before and while reading it? **Skills boost 2** How do I question the text after reading it? **Skills boost 3** How do I consider different readings of the text?	• Not comfortable with the idea of alternative interpretations of a text; may not appreciate that readers bring their own background and experience to bear on the text. (10th Step) • In texts where there are multiple competing meanings or narrative perspectives, may struggle to pinpoint the writer's intention or effects on the reader. (11th Step)	AO1 Identify and interpret explicit and implicit information and ideas	*Far from the Madding Crowd* by Thomas Hardy, 1874 Paper 1
Unit 2 Analysing a text **Skills boost 1** How do I choose what to analyse? **Skills boost 2** How do I structure my analysis? **Skills boost 3** How do I develop my analysis?	• Finds it difficult to synthesise information succinctly or to balance summary responses with more detailed analysis of selected features of a text. (10th Step) • May be limited by formulaic analytical structures, e.g. PEE (point, evidence, explanation). (11th Step) • In more prosaic texts, may struggle to develop analysis beyond identifying a connection between the writer's choices and intention. (11th Step)	AO1 Select and synthesise evidence AO2 Explain, comment on and analyse how writers use language and structure to achieve effects and influence readers	*This Boy's Life* by Tobias Wolff, 1989 Paper 2
Unit 3 Commenting on language **Skills boost 1** How do I focus my comments on language? **Skills boost 2** How do I develop my comments on language? **Skills boost 3** How do I comment on tone?	• May not appreciate the layers of meaning created through imagery or symbolism. (10th Step) • May find it difficult to consider a range of alternative interpretations e.g. how imagery can evoke different responses from different readers. (11th Step) • Understands the need for 'close analysis' of particular language features e.g. student has been told to 'say a lot about a little' but may not know how to achieve this. (12th Step)	AO2 Explain, comment on and analyse how writers use language and structure to achieve effects and influence readers	*The Story of My Life* by Helen Keller, 1903 Paper 2
Unit 4 Commenting on structure **Skills boost 1** How do I comment on whole text structure? **Skills boost 2** How do I identify the impact that sentence structure can have? **Skills boost 3** How do I comment on the writer's use of structure?	• May find it difficult to hold the structure of a whole text in mind, for example the way themes, plot or characters are developed across a lengthy text. (10th Step) • May still find it hard to see how structural choices relate to the presentation of themes and characters. (12th Step) • Understands the need for 'close analysis' of particular language features e.g. student has been told to 'say a lot about a little' but may not know how to achieve this. (12th Step)	AO2 Explain, comment on and analyse how writers use language and structure to achieve effects and influence readers	*Social Media is Making Us Depressed* by Janet Street-Porter, *The Independent* 2016 Paper 2

Unit title and skills boost	Pearson Progression Scale: Barriers (difficulties students may encounter when working towards this step)	Assessment Objectives	Texts used and paper covered
Unit 5 Commenting on language and structure **Skills boost 1** How do I choose the right evidence from the text? **Skills boost 2** How do I build a comment on language and structure? **Skills boost 3** How do I comment on patterns of language and structure?	• May find it difficult to hold the structure of a whole text in mind, for example the way themes, plot or characters are developed across a lengthy text. (10th Step) • May still find it hard to see how structural choices relate to the presentation of themes and characters. (12th Step) • Understands the need for 'close analysis' of particular language features e.g. student has been told to 'say a lot about a little' but may not know how to achieve this. (12th Step)	AO2 Explain, comment on and analyse how writers use language and structure to achieve effects and influence readers	*Adventures in Numberland* by Alex Bellos, 2010 Paper 2
Unit 6 Evaluating texts **Skills boost 1** What makes a text successful? **Skills boost 2** Do I analyse or evaluate? **Skills boost 3** How do I structure an evaluation?	• Finds it difficult to synthesise information succinctly or to balance summary responses with more detailed analysis of selected features of a text. (10th Step) • May be limited by formulaic analytical structures, e.g. PEE (point, evidence, explanation). (11th Step) • In more prosaic texts, may struggle to develop analysis beyond identifying a connection between the writer's choices and intention. (11th Step)	AO4 Evaluate texts critically	*Canterville Ghost* by Oscar Wilde, 1887 Paper 1
Unit 7 Synthesising and comparing **Skills boost 1** How do I synthesise key points? **Skills boost 2** How do I compare synthesised points? **Skills boost 3** How do I structure my comparison?	• Finds it difficult to synthesise information succinctly or to balance summary responses with more detailed analysis of selected features of a text. (10th Step) • In longer, dense or complex texts, may struggle to separate main points from supporting detail. (11th Step)	AO1 Select and synthesise evidence from different texts	*Features of Piltdown Skull: Deliberate Fakes,* The Guardian 1953 *Exploded: the myth of a miracle bomb detector,* Ben Goldacre, *The Guardian* 2009 Paper 2
Unit 8 Comparing ideas and perspectives **Skills boost 1** How do I identify relevant ideas and perspectives? **Skills boost 2** How do I compare ideas and perspectives? **Skills boost 3** How do I develop my comparison?	• May struggle to make close comparisons of the writers' choices at word, sentence or whole text level and explore how they support the writers' likely intentions. (10th Step) • May be reluctant to incorporate fully developed analysis of a writer's choices if it does not appear immediately relevant to the broader comparison being made. (11th Step)	AO3 Compare writers' ideas and perspectives, as well as how these are conveyed	*All Things Wise and Wonderful* by James Herriot, 1977 *H is for Hawk* by Helen MacDonald, 2014 Paper 2
Unit 9 Expressing your ideas clearly and precisely **Skills boost 1** How do I express my ideas concisely? **Skills boost 2** How do I express my ideas precisely? **Skills boost 3** How do I express my ideas clearly?	• May be limited by formulaic analytical structures, e.g. PEE (point, evidence, explanation). (11th Step) • Can equate quality with length or wealth of detail and find it difficult to write with precision and succinctness. (12th step)	AO1 Identify and interpret explicit and implicit information and ideas	*Vanity Fair* by Makepeace Thackeray, 1848 Paper 1
More practice texts	**Three** additional extracts referenced in the additional exam-style question provided at the end of each unit.		*Nicholas Nickleby* by Charles Dickens, 1835 *English Journey* by J.B. Priestley, 1933 *A Window on Warsaw* by Lynda Bailey, *The Daily Telegraph* 2009

① Tackling an unseen text

This unit will help you tackle the unseen texts that you will encounter in your exams. The skills you will build are to:

- question the text before reading
- think about the whole text after reading
- consider different readings of the text.

In the exam, you will face questions like the ones below. These are about the text on page 2. At the end of the unit, you will write your own response to these questions.

Exam-style question

1. From lines 15–21, identify **one** phrase which suggests that Gabriel Oak is not a confident person. (1 mark)

2. From lines 4–14, identify **two** phrases which suggest something about Bathsheba Everdene's personality. (2 marks)

The three key questions in the **skills boosts** will help you tackle an unseen text.

 How do I question the text before and while reading it?

 How do I question the text after reading it?

 How do I consider different readings of the text?

Read the extract on page 2, taken from the novel *Far from the Madding Crowd* by Thomas Hardy, first published in 1874. You will tackle a 19th-century fiction extract in the Reading section of your Paper 1 exam.

As you read, remember the following:

Before reading the extract, carefully read any introduction provided. It is intended to help you understand where the text is taken from, why it was written and other useful background information you might need.

While reading the extract, if you lose understanding of the text, stop and reread from the last sentence or paragraph that you clearly understood.

After reading the extract, read it again.

In this extract from *Far from the Madding Crowd*, Gabriel Oak, a farmer, has come to Mrs Hurst's house to propose marriage to her niece, Bathsheba Everdene.

Text 1 Far from the Madding Crowd, Thomas Hardy

"Will you come in, Mr. Oak?"

"Oh, thank 'ee," said Gabriel, following her to the fireplace. "I've brought a lamb for Miss Everdene. I thought she might like one to rear; girls do."

"She might," said Mrs. Hurst, musingly; "though she's only a visitor here. If you will wait a minute, Bathsheba will
5   be in."

"Yes, I will wait," said Gabriel, sitting down. "The lamb isn't really the business I came about, Mrs. Hurst. In short, I was going to ask her if she'd like to be married."

"And were you indeed?"

"Yes. Because if she would, I should be very glad to marry her. D'ye know if she's got any other young man hanging
10   about her at all?"

"Let me think," said Mrs. Hurst, poking the fire **superfluously**… "Yes – bless you, ever so many young men. You see, Farmer Oak, she's so good-looking, and an excellent scholar besides – she was going to be a governess once, you know, only she was too wild. Not that her young men ever come here – but, Lord, in the nature of women, she must have a dozen!"

15   "That's unfortunate," said Farmer Oak, contemplating a crack in the stone floor with sorrow. "I'm only an every-day sort of man, and my only chance was in being the first comer… Well, there's no use in my waiting, for that was all I came about: so I'll take myself off home-along, Mrs. Hurst."

When Gabriel had gone about two hundred yards along the down, he heard a "hoi-hoi!" uttered behind him, in a piping note of more treble quality than that in which the exclamation usually embodies itself when shouted across
20   a field. He looked round, and saw a girl racing after him, waving a white handkerchief.

Oak stood still – and the runner drew nearer. It was Bathsheba Everdene. Gabriel's colour deepened: hers was already deep, not, as it appeared, from emotion, but from running.

"Farmer Oak – I —" she said, pausing for want of breath pulling up in front of him with a slanted face and putting her hand to her side.

25   "I have just called to see you," said Gabriel, pending her further speech.

"Yes – I know that," she said panting like a robin, her face red and moist from her exertions, like a peony petal before the sun dries off the dew. "I didn't know you had come to ask to have me, or I should have come in from the garden instantly. I ran after you to say – that my aunt made a mistake in sending you away from courting me —"

Gabriel expanded. "I'm sorry to have made you run so fast, my dear," he said, with a grateful sense of favours to
30   come. "Wait a bit till you've found your breath."

"– It was quite a mistake – aunt's telling you I had a young man already," Bathsheba went on. "I haven't a sweetheart at all – and I never had one, and I thought that, as times go with women, it was SUCH a pity to send you away thinking that I had several."

"Really and truly I am glad to hear that!" said Farmer Oak, smiling one of his long special smiles, and blushing with
35   gladness. He held out his hand to take hers, which, when she had eased her side by pressing it there, was prettily extended upon her bosom to still her loud-beating heart. Directly he seized it she put it behind her, so that it slipped through his fingers like an eel.

superfluously: unnecessarily

How do I question the text before and while reading it?

Questioning the text will help you understand and explore what you are reading and your response to it. This is perfect preparation for a high-level analysis of the text.

① Think about your expectations **before you read** the text and whether they were confirmed or how they changed **while you were reading** the text. Note down 🖊 some ideas in the spaces below.

The characters	The events described	The ideas explored
Before reading I expected	Before reading I expected	Before reading I expected
While reading I realised	While reading I realised	While reading I realised

② **a** What questions occurred to you as you read the text? They might have been about the characters, events or ideas in the extract. Note down 🖊 **two** of them below.

Question 1: ....

....

Question 2: ....

....

b Choose **one** of the questions you noted above. How might the writer have **encouraged** you to ask that question as you read the text? Write 🖊 two or three sentences explaining your ideas.

....

....

....

....

③ Look at the title of a 21st-century non-fiction text: a newspaper article published in 2016.

Social media is making us depressed: let's learn to turn it off

What expectations might you have and what questions might you ask of this text? 🖊

....

....

....

....

② How do I question the text after reading it?

After you have read the text, reread it, thinking carefully about how the writer has written it and why.

① Read the text on page 2 again, thinking about its **structure**. Write 🖉 two or three sentences to summarise how the characters, events and/or ideas in the text change and develop.

You could use sentence starters like these to help you:

| At the start of the extract... | However, when... | By the end of the extract... |

....

....

....

....

② a Note down 🖉 **two** different ways in which you might expect the story of Gabriel and Bathsheba to develop.

Development 1: ....

....

Development 2: ....

....

b For each idea, note down 🖉 **how** the writer might have created those expectations. Is it through:

- what the characters say and do • the ways in which the narrator tells their story
- the writer's choices of vocabulary and/or sentence structure?

....

....

....

....

c Now think about **why** the writer might have created the expectations you noted above. Was it:

- to engage the reader's interest • to manipulate the reader's response to the characters
- to mislead the reader • or for another reason?

Add notes 🖉 to extend your ideas below.

....

....

....

....

....

3 How do I consider different readings of the text?

Different readers may respond very differently to the same text. During and after reading, think about how others may respond differently to you – and why.

1 Look at some of the different reactions that readers have had to the character of Gabriel Oak in this extract.

A.
> Oak is shy and gentle and innocent. I feel sorry for him.

B.
> Oak is a gullible fool who deserves to have his heart broken.

C.
> Oak is quiet and determined and willing to risk humiliating himself. I admire him.

a Look at the extract on page 2 again. Identify at least one piece of evidence to support each of these points of view, underlining (A) and labelling it (✏) A, B or C.

b Which of the three points of view above do you agree with most strongly? Write (✏) a sentence or two to explain your choice.

....

....

....

2 a How might different readers respond differently to the character of Bathsheba Everdene in the extract? Write down (✏) your thoughts in the speech bubbles below.

b Write (✏) two or three sentences beneath each speech bubble, to explain why a reader might respond in this way.

Reader A

Reader B

....

....

....

....

....

....

....

Tackling an unseen text

When you tackle an unseen text you need to:

- Think about your expectations of the text based on the kind of text it is, when it was written, its title, its subject matter and any other information you are given.
- Read the text very carefully, comparing your responses to the text with your expectations.
- Think about how and why the writer might have created or manipulated your expectations of, and response to, the text.
- Think about how other readers might respond differently to the text.

Some of the questions you will face in your exams are designed to test your skill in extracting **explicit** and **implicit** information from an unseen text. Once you have read the text and explored your response, you will be ready to tackle these kinds of question.

> **explicit** clearly stated
> **implicit** implied; not clearly stated

Look at one student's responses to these exam-style questions.

Exam-style question

1. From lines 31–39, identify **one** piece of information that suggests Bathsheba Everdene may not agree to marry Gabriel Oak. **(1 mark)**

2. From lines 31–39, identify **two** pieces of information that suggest Gabriel Oak is anxious to marry Bathsheba Everdene. **(2 marks)**

---

1. Mrs Hurst said that Bathsheba had lots of sweethearts, but Bathsheba says, "I haven't a sweetheart at all", which makes me think she is deceitful and may be leading Gabriel on.

2. Gabriel has 'a grateful sense of favours to come', as though he is expecting her to agree to marry him and he says he is 'Really and truly ...glad to hear' that Bathsheba has no other sweethearts at all.

---

(1) Which of this student's answers are correct? Write down ✏ two or three sentences to explain your ideas.

....

....

....

....

....

....

....

....

....

....

....

....

Your turn!

After you have read and understood the text, identified its key points and explored the writer's intention, you are ready to tackle **all of the questions** you are likely to be asked in your exam.

Test your knowledge with the exam-style questions below.

5 "She might," said Mrs. Hurst, musingly; "though she's only a visitor here. If you will wait a minute, Bathsheba will be in."

"Yes, I will wait," said Gabriel, sitting down. "The lamb isn't really the business I came about, Mrs. Hurst. In short, I was going to ask her if she'd like to be married."

"And were you indeed?"

"Yes. Because if she would, I should be very glad to marry her. D'ye know if she's got any other young man hanging
10 about her at all?"

"Let me think," said Mrs. Hurst, poking the fire **superfluously**… "Yes -- bless you, ever so many young men. You see, Farmer Oak, she's so good-looking, and an excellent scholar besides – she was going to be a governess once, you know, only she was too wild. Not that her young men ever come here – but, Lord, in the nature of women, she must have a dozen!"

15 "That's unfortunate," said Farmer Oak, contemplating a crack in the stone floor with sorrow. "I'm only an every-day sort of man, and my only chance was in being the first comer… Well, there's no use in my waiting, for that was all I came about: so I'll take myself off home-along, Mrs. Hurst."

When Gabriel had gone about two hundred yards along the down, he heard a "hoi-hoi!" uttered behind him, in a piping note of more treble quality than that in which the exclamation usually embodies itself when shouted across
20 a field. He looked round, and saw a girl racing after him, waving a white handkerchief.

Exam-style question

1. From lines 15–20, identify **one** phrase which suggests that Gabriel Oak is not a confident person. (1 mark)

....

....

2. From lines 4–14, identify **two** phrases which suggest something about the character of Bathsheba Everdene.

You may use your own words or quotation from the text. (2 marks)

1. ....

....

2. ....

....

Review your skills

Check up

Review your response to the exam-style question on page 7. Tick ✓ the column to show how well you think you have done each of the following.

	Not quite ✓	Nearly there ✓	Got it! ✓
questioned the text before and while reading it	☐	☐	☐
questioned the text after reading it	☐	☐	☐
considered different readings of the text	☐	☐	☐

Look over all of your work in this unit. Note down ✐ the three most important things to remember when you first read an unseen text.

1. ....

2. ....

3. ....

Need more practice?

Here is another exam-style question, this time relating to Text B on page 74: an extract from *English Journey* by J.B. Priestley. You'll find some suggested points to refer to in the Answers section.

Exam-style question

1. From **lines 1–5**, identify **one** reason the writer thinks that the *Mauretania* is 'remarkable'.

(1 mark)

....

....

2. From **lines 6–17**, give **two** examples that show how Jarrow has changed. (2 marks)

1. ....

2. ....

How confident do you feel about each of these **skills?** Colour ✐ in the bars.

❶ How do I question the text before and while reading?
☐☐☐☐

❷ How do I question the text after reading it?
☐☐☐☐

❸ How do I consider different readings of the text?
☐☐☐☐

Select and synthesise evidence (AO1)
Explain, comment on and analyse how writers use language
and structure to achieve effects and influence readers (AO2)

② Analysing a text

This unit will help you analyse a text, a skill you will need to demonstrate in **all** the longer answers you have to write in your exams. The skills you will build are to:

- identify key elements for analysis in a text
- structure your analysis
- develop your analysis.

In the exam you will face questions like the one below. This is about the text on page 10. At the end of the unit you will write your own response to this question.

Exam-style question

Analyse how the writer uses language and structure to interest and engage readers.

Support your views with detailed reference to the text.

(15 marks)

The three key questions in the **skills boosts** will help you analyse the text.

| ① How do I choose what to analyse? | ② How do I structure my analysis? | ③ How do I develop my analysis? |

Read the extract on page 10 from *This Boy's Life* by Tobias Wolff, an autobiography published in 1989. You will tackle a 20th-century non-fiction extract in the Reading section of your Paper 2 exam.

As you read, remember the following: ✓

Remember the focus of the exam question you are preparing to respond to.

Think about the ways in which the writer tries to interest and engage readers.

Underline Ⓐ or tick ✓ any parts of the text that **you** find engaging or interesting.

In the opening of his autobiography, the writer describes the journey when he and his mother moved from Florida to Utah.

Text 1 This Boy's Life, Tobias Wolff

Our car boiled over again just after my mother and I crossed the **Continental Divide**. While we were waiting for it to cool we heard, from somewhere above us, the bawling of an airhorn. The sound got louder and then a big truck came around the comer and shot past us into the next curve, its trailer shimmying wildly. We stared after it. "Oh, Toby," my mother said, "he's lost his brakes."

5   The sound of the horn grew distant, then faded in the wind that sighed in the trees all around us.

By the time we got there, quite a few people were standing along the cliff where the truck went over. It had smashed through the guardrails and fallen hundreds of feet through empty space to the river below, where it lay on its back among the boulders. It looked pitifully small. A stream of thick black smoke rose from the cab, feathering out in the wind. My mother asked whether anyone had gone to report the accident. Someone had. We
10   stood with the others at the cliff's edge. Nobody spoke. My mother put her arm around my shoulder.

For the rest of the day she kept looking over at me, touching me, brushing back my hair. I saw that the time was right to make a play for souvenirs. I knew she had no money for them, and I had tried not to ask, but now that her guard was down I couldn't help myself. When we pulled out of Grand Junction I owned a beaded Indian belt, beaded moccasins, and a bronze horse with a removable, tooled-leather saddle.

15   It was 1955 and we were driving from Florida to Utah, to get away from a man my mother was afraid of and to get rich on **uranium**. We were going to change our luck.

We'd left Sarasota in the dead of summer, right after my tenth birthday, and headed West under low flickering skies that turned black and exploded and cleared just long enough to leave the air gauzy with steam. We drove through Georgia, Alabama, Tennessee, Kentucky, stopping to cool the engine in towns where people moved with
20   arthritic slowness and spoke in thick, strangled tongues. Idlers with rotten teeth surrounded the car to press peanuts on the pretty Yankee lady and her little boy, arguing among themselves about shortcuts. Women looked up from their flower beds as we drove past, or watched us from their porches, sometimes impassively, sometimes giving us a nod and a flutter of their fans.

Every couple of hours the Nash Rambler boiled over. My mother kept digging into her little **grubstake** but no
25   mechanic could fix it. All we could do was wait for it to cool, then drive on until it boiled over again. (My mother came to hate this machine so much that not long after we got to Utah she gave it away to a woman she met in a cafeteria.) At night we slept in boggy rooms where headlight beams crawled up and down the walls and mosquitoes sang in our ears, incessant as the tires whining on the highway outside. But none of this bothered me. I was caught up in my mother's freedom, her delight in her freedom, her dream of transformation.

Continental Divide: a line of mountainous land that divides the United States in two: rivers to the east of the Divide drain into the Atlantic; rivers to the west drain into the Pacific Ocean
uranium: a valuable metal used in the nuclear power and arms industry
grubstake: the savings she had put aside for their new life

How do I choose what to analyse?

A writer may have several intentions when they write a text – but none are more important than the intention to interest and engage the reader. One way to begin the process of analysing a text is to identify elements of the text where the writer has made a significant attempt to achieve this.

Look again at the exam-style question you are exploring:

Exam-style question

Analyse how the writer uses language and structure to interest and engage readers.

Support your views with detailed reference to the text.

(15 marks)

1. Which of the elements below has the writer of the text on page 10 used to interest and engage the reader? Tick ✓ any that you can identify, and label ✏ the relevant area of the extract A, B, C, etc.

A. Interesting or unusual characters, settings, ideas or facts	B. Sudden changes in character, argument, or tone	C. Dramatic events or moments of tension
D. Twists, shocks or surprises	E. Description of a scene or situation	F. Humour

These can be relevant to both fiction and non-fiction texts.

2. Now look more closely at the key elements of the text you have identified. Which of the features below has the writer used in those elements? Underline Ⓐ and label ✏ them in the extract on page 10.

a Significant structural choices

i a non-chronological account of events

ii a dramatic opening

iii a surprising or shocking ending

iv withholding then revealing significant information

v contrasting two or more ideas, characters or events

vi any other significant structural choices you can identify

b Significant paragraph or sentence structures

i short, dramatic or emphatic paragraphs or sentences

ii minor sentences (which contain no verbs)

iii long sentences where a number of clauses build detail or atmosphere

v sentences listing a sequence of events or ideas

vi any other significant sentence structures you can identify

c Rich vocabulary choices

i language with significant connotations or implications

ii vivid, descriptive language

iiii emotive, shocking or dramatic language

iv persuasive or emphatic language

v formal and/or informal language

vi any other rich vocabulary choices you can identify

2 How do I structure my analysis?

Every point you make in an analysis should be supported with evidence from the text and analytical comment. However, following a rigid structure – such as writing in point-evidence-explanation (PEE) paragraphs – can limit the range and depth of your analysis.

Read the sentences below. They are taken from one paragraph of a student's analysis of the extract.

A.
The writer begins the extract with a dramatic incident, taken out of chronological order to engage the reader's interest immediately.

B.
The narrator hears "the bawling of an air horn" and describes how a "big truck… shot past us… its trailer shimmying wildly."

C.
When we next see the truck, it has "smashed through the guardrails" of the road and "fallen hundreds of feet through empty space."

D.
The personification of the truck lying "on its back" suggests the 'death' of the truck and the almost certain death of its driver, adding to the reader's sense of shock.

E.
The writer summarises the impact of the incident in the short, emphatic sentence: "Nobody spoke."

(1) Think about the function of each of the sentences above. Some may have more than one function.

  a Write P ✎ beside any of the sentences that makes a **point**.

  b Write Q ✎ beside any of the sentences that includes a **quotation**.

  c Write A ✎ beside any of the sentences that **analyses** the text.

(2) **a** Which of the sentences would you include in a paragraph of analysis focusing on the truck accident? Tick ✓ them.

  b How would you sequence the sentences you have ticked? Number them ✎ in your order.

  c How would you summarise the structure of the paragraph you have sequenced?
Use 'point', 'quotation' and 'analysis' in your summary.

....

....

....

....

....

3 How do I develop my analysis?

To produce an effective analysis, you should aim to make your comments as detailed and specific as you can. Think about:

- commenting on the writer's choices – why the writer made them and how the writer has used them
- being precise about the impact of the writer's choices on the reader.

① Look at this quotation and comment from one student's analysis of the fourth paragraph of the extract on page 10.

> The writer finishes the paragraph by describing the souvenirs his mother bought for him to take his mind off the truck accident: "When we pulled out of Grand Junction I owned a beaded Indian belt, beaded moccasins, and a bronze horse with a removable, tooled-leather saddle". This creates humour.

You can develop an analysis by thinking carefully about all the writer's choices. Look at the second paragraph of the extract and answer these questions to develop ideas you could add to the paragraph above.

a How does the quoted sentence's position in the paragraph add to its impact on the reader?

....
....
....

b How does the structure of this sentence add to its impact?

....
....
....

c How do the writer's vocabulary choices add to its impact?

....
....
....

d Why has the writer made these choices of paragraph, sentence structure and vocabulary?

....
....
....
....

e How does this paragraph relate to the previous section of the text?

....
....
....
....

Analysing a text

To write an effective analysis you need to do the following:

- Focus closely on the key words in the question: what are you being asked to analyse?
- Identify key elements of the text for analysis.
- Structure and develop your analysis, exploring the writer's choices and their impact on the reader.

Look at the exam-style question.

Exam-style question

Analyse how the writer uses language and structure to interest and engage readers.

Support your views with detailed reference to the text.

(15 marks)

(1) Look at this paragraph from one student's response to the exam-style question above.

> The writer explains why he and his mother are moving: to "get away from a man my mother was afraid of and to get rich on uranium". The writer does not give any more detail about this man, which makes him seem even more threatening and sinister.

Think carefully about the comments you could add to the paragraph. You could use the questions on page 13 to help you. Note down (✐) some ideas below.

....

....

....

....

....

(2) How would you sequence the paragraph? Number (✐) your ideas above, and rewrite (✐) the paragraph below, developing the analysis as fully as possible.

....

....

....

....

....

....

....

....

Your turn!

You are now going to write ✏ your own answer in response to the exam-style question.

Exam-style question

Analyse how the writer uses language and structure to interest and engage readers.

Support your views with detailed reference to the text.

(15 marks)

1 Reread the final two paragraphs of the extract, from lines 26–29. Which ideas, event or element of the text could your paragraph of analysis focus on? Note down ✏ some possible ideas below.

....

....

....

....

....

....

....

2 Which of your possible ideas would allow you to write the most developed analysis? Choose one of your ideas above and underline Ⓐ it.

3 Now think about how you will develop your analysis of the idea, event or element of the text you have chosen to focus on and note down ✏ your ideas below. Think about:

- the position of your chosen focus in the text
- how this element relates to other elements of the text
- the writer's choice of paragraph and sentence structure
- the writer's vocabulary choices
- the impact that the writer intends his choices to have on the reader.

4 How will you sequence your paragraph? Number ✏ all the ideas you noted above.

5 Now write ✏ one paragraph of developed analysis in response to the exam-style question on paper.

Review your skills

Check up

Review your response to the exam-style question on page 15. Tick ✓ the column to show how well you think you have done each of the following.

	Not quite ✓	Nearly there ✓	Got it! ✓
selected elements of the text for analysis	☐	☐	☐
structured my analysis	☐	☐	☐
developed my analysis	☐	☐	☐

Look over all of your work in this unit. Note down ✐ the three most important things to remember when you analyse the text.

1. ....

2. ....

3. ....

Need more practice?

Here is another exam-style question, this time relating to Text A on page 73: an extract from *Nicholas Nickleby* by Charles Dickens. You'll find some suggested points to refer to in the Answers section.

Exam-style question

In the first paragraph, how does the writer use language and structure to create a humorous description of the scene?

Support your views with reference to the text.

(6 marks)

How confident do you feel about each of these **skills?** Colour ✐ in the bars.

1 How do I choose what to analyse?

2 How do I structure my analysis?

3 How do I develop my analysis?

③ Commenting on language

This unit will help you comment on a writer's use of language. The skills you will build are to:

- identify and explore patterns of language choice in a text
- explore layers of meaning and a variety of responses to the writer's language choices
- identify and comment on the writer's use of tone.

In the exam you will face questions like the one below. This is about the text on page 18. This unit will prepare you to write your own response to this question, focusing on the writer's use of language. Unit 4 focuses on how to analyse the writer's use of structure.

Exam-style question

Analyse how the writer uses language and structure to interest and engage readers.

Support your views with detailed reference to the text.

(15 marks)

The three key questions in the **skills boosts** will help you comment on language.

① How do I focus my comments on language?

② How do I develop my comments on language?

③ How do I comment on tone?

Read the extract on page 18 from *The Story of My Life* by Helen Keller, first published in 1903. You will tackle a 20th-century non-fiction extract in the Reading section of your Paper 2 exam.

As you read, remember the following: ✓

| Remember the focus of the exam question you are preparing to respond to. | Think about the ways in which the writer tries to interest and engage readers and any language choices that contribute to that intention. | Underline Ⓐ or tick ✓ any parts of the text that **you** find significant or interesting. |

Helen Keller was born in 1880. At the age of 19 months she contracted a fever that left her unable to hear, see or speak. In this extract from her autobiography, she describes how, when she was nearly seven, her teacher, Anne Sullivan, changed her life.

Text 1 The Story of My Life, Helen Keller

The morning after my teacher came she led me into her room and gave me a doll. When I had played with it a little while, Miss Sullivan slowly spelled into my hand the word "d-o-l-l." I was at once interested in this finger play and tried to imitate it. When I finally succeeded in making the letters correctly I was flushed with childish pleasure and pride. I did not know that I was spelling a word or even that words existed; I was simply making my fingers
5   go in monkey-like imitation. In the days that followed I learned to spell in this uncomprehending way a great many words, among them *pin*, *hat*, *cup* and a few verbs like *sit*, *stand* and *walk*. But my teacher had been with me several weeks before I understood that everything has a name.

One day, while I was playing with my new doll, Miss Sullivan put my big rag doll into my lap also, spelled "d-o-l-l" and tried to make me understand that "d-o-l-l" applied to both. Earlier in the day we had had a
10 tussle over the words "m-u-g" and "w-a-t-e-r." Miss Sullivan had tried to impress it upon me that "m-u-g" is *mug* and that "w-a-t-e-r" is *water*, but I persisted in confounding the two. In despair she had dropped the subject for the time, only to renew it at the first opportunity. I became impatient at her repeated attempts and, seizing the new doll, I dashed it upon the floor. I was keenly delighted when I felt the fragments of the broken doll at my feet. Neither sorrow nor regret followed my passionate outburst. I had not loved the doll. In the still,
15 dark world in which I lived there was no strong sentiment of tenderness. I felt my teacher sweep the fragments to one side of the hearth, and I had a sense of satisfaction that the cause of my discomfort was removed. She brought me my hat, and I knew I was going out into the warm sunshine. This thought, if a wordless sensation may be called a thought, made me hop and skip with pleasure.

We walked down the path to the **well-house**, attracted by the fragrance of the honeysuckle with which it
20 was covered. Some one was **drawing water** and my teacher placed my hand under the spout. As the cool stream gushed over one hand she spelled into the other the word water, first slowly, then rapidly. I stood still, my whole attention fixed upon the motions of her fingers. Suddenly I felt a misty consciousness as of something forgotten–a thrill of returning thought; and somehow the mystery of language was revealed to me. I knew then that "w-a-t-e-r" meant the wonderful cool something that was flowing over my hand. That living word
25 awakened my soul, gave it light, hope, joy, set it free! There were barriers still, it is true, but barriers that could in time be swept away.

I left the well-house eager to learn. Everything had a name, and each name gave birth to a new thought. As we returned to the house every object which I touched seemed to quiver with life. That was because I saw everything with the strange, new sight that had come to me. On entering the door I remembered the doll I had broken. I felt
30 my way to the hearth and picked up the pieces. I tried vainly to put them together. Then my eyes filled with tears; for I realized what I had done, and for the first time I felt repentance and sorrow.

well-house: a small building containing a water well
drawing water: pumping water from the well

1 How do I focus my comments on language?

When you first consider the writer's language choices in any text, look for patterns of language that create similar or contrasting characters, situations, thoughts or feelings. You can then explore how individual language choices contribute to the impact of these patterns on the text and on the reader.

1 Which of the following pairs of ideas are presented as similar or contrasting in the text on page 18? Draw lines 🖉 to link them – then add 🖉 any of your own ideas.

The writer and her teacher	The writer's house and the outside world	
The writer's thoughts and feelings at the beginning and at the end of the text	Before and after the writer understands how language describes the world	

2 Look at some quotations from Text 1 below. Draw 🖉 lines linking any quotations that are similar or contrasting in their ideas and/or the writer's use of language.

A.
"I was keenly delighted when I felt the fragments of the broken doll at my feet. Neither sorrow nor regret followed my passionate outburst." (lines 13–14)

B.
"In the still, dark world in which I lived there was no strong sentiment of tenderness." (lines 14–15)

C.
"I knew I was going out into the warm sunshine. This thought … made me hop and skip with pleasure." (lines 18–19)

D.
"That living word awakened my soul, gave it light, hope, joy, set it free!" (lines 24–25)

E.
"every object which I touched seemed to quiver with life" (line 28)

F.
"my eyes filled with tears; for I realized what I had done, and for the first time I felt repentance and sorrow." (lines 30–31)

3 Choose one pair of quotations from question 2 that you have linked. Now circle Ⓐ any of the writer's language choices in those quotations that create a similarity or a contrast.

4 Write 🖉 a sentence or two explaining why you chose the two quotations and the language choices you have circled and linked.

....

....

....

....

....

....

2 How do I develop my comments on language?

You can explore a text by considering a range of possible meanings, readings, interpretations and responses — and the ways in which the writer's use of language supports them.

① Look carefully at these sentences from the extract on page 18.

> I knew then that "w-a-t-e-r" meant the wonderful cool something that was flowing over my hand. That living word awakened my soul, gave it light, hope, joy, set it free!

a Choose **one** word or phrase from the sentences above that you feel is particularly rich in meaning. Some words have been highlighted to help you choose.

b Note down 🖉 at least **two** different ideas, connotations or implications that your chosen word or phrase suggests to you.

....

....

....

....

....

② Look carefully at this short extract from the text on page 18. Think about the different responses that the writer is trying to create.

> … seizing the new doll, I dashed it upon the floor. I was keenly delighted when I felt the fragments of the broken doll at my feet. Neither sorrow nor regret followed my passionate outburst. I had not loved the doll. In the still, dark world in which I lived there was no strong sentiment of tenderness.

a Think about ways in which the writer encourages the reader to feel **antipathy** for her behaviour in this part of the text. Circle Ⓐ any language choices that contribute to this response.

> **antipathy**: the opposite of sympathy — to dislike or feel hostility

b Now think about ways in which the writer encourages the reader to feel sympathy for her. Underline Ⓐ any language choices that contribute to this response.

c Why might the writer have intended to encourage both of these very different responses in the reader? Write 🖉 a sentence or two explaining your ideas.

....

....

....

....

....

How do I comment on tone?

The writer's language choices help to create the tone of a piece of writing: the mood the writer aims to create or the voice they use to express their ideas.

① Look at some students' comments on the tone that the writer creates at different points in the text on page 18.

A. ☐ The writer creates a tone of calm and peacefulness.

B. ☐ The writer creates a tone of excitement.

C. ☐ The writer creates a tone of self-pity.

D. ☐ The writer creates a tone of astonishment and surprise.

E. ☐ The writer creates a tone of anger and frustration.

F. ☐ The writer creates a tone of fear and menace.

G. ☐ The writer creates a tone of disappointment.

H. ☐ The writer creates a tone of solemnity and sadness.

a Which of these statements do you agree with? Tick ✓ them.

b For **each** of the statements you ticked above, identify **one** part of the text on page 18 where the writer achieves that tone. Mark and label ✎ the relevant part of the text to identify it; for example, you could write 'calm' or 'self-pity', etc.

c Now look closely at the parts of the text you have marked and labelled. Circle Ⓐ **two or more** words or phrases in that part of the text that contribute to the tone you have identified.

d Write ✎ two or three sentences about the tone of **one** part of the text. Aim to comment on:

- how the writer's language choices contribute to the tone you have identified
- the impact of that tone on the reader.

....

....

....

....

....

....

....

....

....

....

Unit 3 Commenting on language   **21**

Commenting on language

To comment on language as fully and effectively as possible, you need to consider:

- how and why the writer creates patterns of language
- the impact of specific language choices within those patterns
- the range of meanings, interpretations and responses the writer may have intended
- how the writer's language choices contribute to the tone of their writing.

Look at this exam-style question:

Exam-style question

Analyse how the writer uses language and structure to interest and engage readers.

Support your views with detailed reference to the text.

(15 marks)

(1) Look at this paragraph from one student's response to the question.

Identifies a pattern of language use

Focuses on the impact of the writer's language choices on the reader

> At the start of this part of the text, the writer focuses on her sense of smell and touch: the "fragrance of the honeysuckle" and the "cool stream". The positive connotations of "fragrance" and "cool" suggest pleasure within the limitations of her blindness and deafness. However, these limitations are soon forgotten as she effectively conveys her thoughts and feelings when she understands the purpose and the power of language. The writer contrasts the vagueness of her "misty consciousness" and the "mystery of language" with the excited, joyous tone of the "thrill" she feels when language is "revealed" to her. The writer's language choices could simply suggest her joy; however, they could also strongly suggest the sense of unconsciousness and imprisonment she felt before she was "awakened" and "set free", creating a mixture of possible responses in the reader from sympathy to elation.

Comments on tone

Explores a range of meanings and/ or responses

Can you identify the different features of this student's response? Underline (A) or highlight  the relevant parts of the paragraph then link (✏) the annotations to them.

Your turn!

You are now going to write your own answer in response to the exam-style question.

Exam-style question

Analyse how the writer uses language and structure to interest and engage readers.

Support your views with detailed reference to the text.

(15 marks)

In your answer, remember to consider the writer's use of language.

(1) Use the space below to gather, organise and note down 🖉 your ideas.

Patterns of language choice
You could think about patterns in the writer's language choices when she describes:
- her thought and feelings
- her struggle to learn
- her actions.

Tone
You could think about:
- how the tone of the writer's voice changes or develops
- the tone created at specific points in the text.

A range of responses
You could think about different responses to:
- the writer
- the events described.

(2) Now write 🖉 your response to the exam-style question above on paper.

Review your skills

Check up

Review your response to the exam-style question on page 23. Tick ✓ the column to show how well you think you have done each of the following.

	Not quite ✓	Nearly there ✓	Got it! ✓
identified and explored patterns of language choice	☐	☐	☐
explored layers of meaning and a variety of responses to the writer's language choices	☐	☐	☐
identified and commented on tone	☐	☐	☐

Look over all of your work in this unit. Note 🖉 down the three most important things to remember when commenting language.

1. ....

2. ....

3. ....

Need more practice?

Here is another exam-style question, this time relating to Text B on page 74: an extract from *English Journey* by J.B. Priestley. You'll find some suggested points to refer to in the Answers section.

Exam-style question

Analyse how the writer uses language and structure to interest and engage readers.

Support your views with detailed reference to the text.

(15 marks)

How confident do you feel about each of these **skills?** Colour 🖉 in the bars.

1 How do I focus my comments on language?

2 How do I develop my comments on language?

3 How do I comment on tone?

④ Commenting on structure

This unit will help you comment on structure. The skills you will build are to:

- comment on the writer's use of whole text structure
- comment on the writer's use of sentence structure
- develop and build comments on the writer's structural choices.

In the exam you will face questions like the one below. This is about the text on page 26. At the end of the unit you will write your own response to this question, focusing on the writer's use of structure. Unit 3 focuses on how to analyse the writer's use of language.

Exam-style question

Analyse how the writer uses language and structure to interest and engage readers.

Support your views with detailed reference to the text.

(15 marks)

The three key questions in the **skills boosts** will help you comment on sentence forms.

1 How do I comment on whole text structure?

2 How do I identify the impact that sentence structure can have?

3 How do I comment on the writer's use of structure?

Read the newspaper article on page 26, written by Janet Street-Porter and published in *The Independent* in 2016. You will tackle a 21st century non-fiction extract in the Reading section of your Paper 2 exam.

As you read, remember the following:

Remember the focus of the exam question you are preparing to respond to.

Think about how the writer has selected ideas and structured the text to engage and interest readers.

Think about how the writer has structured the text and her sentences to add impact to those ideas.

This newspaper article appeared in *The Independent* in April 2016.

Text 1 Social media is making us depressed: let's learn to turn it off, Janet Street-Porter

Do Facebook and Twitter make us happier? The answer it would seem is: no. A recent survey found as many as one in five people say they feel depressed as a result of using social media. That might come as a surprise to the generation under 30; social media is part of their DNA and teenagers are rapidly losing the ability to communicate if not through their smartphones. But the stress of constantly monitoring our statuses and endlessly documenting
5   every aspect of our lives via networks like Facebook, Snapchat and Instagram is taking its toll.

Employers claim many school leavers are unprepared for the world of work, where they will have to interact with people outside their peer group and actually speak face-to-face with total strangers.

Meanwhile, there have been countless academic studies since 2015 on the negative impacts of social media, showing that its regular use leads to feelings of anxiety, isolation and low self-esteem, not to mention poor sleep.
10 We use these outlets to present a false picture of our lives to the online community; with flattering selfies and **faux**-glamorous images of holidays, parties and meals. It's as if we're starring in a movie of the life we'd like to lead, not the humdrum one we actually inhabit. An underwhelming number of shares or 'likes' can lead to debilitating feelings of inadequacy.

We post intimate fragments of our lives to total strangers, falsely believing that a 'friend' online is a real friend
15 whose opinions matter. As for Twitter, it is a vehicle for screaming, nothing more and nothing less. Best not to read tweets if you are of a vulnerable disposition.

Recently, I dared to write that cycling was being prioritised over walking in London. Cyclists, like Scottish Nationalists, are the thugs of the new era. Immediately, my words were distorted, and amplified via Twitter. I was accused of hate crimes against cycling even though I carefully said that I actually enjoyed it. I received 1,000 vile
20 and abusive messages – and they're still coming.

Twitter has an effect on one's disposition; augmenting anger and upset. Many of the women I know have come off Twitter because of the constant abuse that waits every time they pick up their phone or log in to their computer.

The latest fashion among hipsters is to have a 'digital-free' home. That could be a good move. Arianna Huffington has just written a book (*The Sleep Revolution*) citing experts who say there should be no screens in the bedroom
25 and we shouldn't use social media in the hour before lights-out.

How many times have we read a message on our phones and then spent hours in turmoil? Social media never switches off: someone, somewhere, is posting pictures, comments or messages, asking you to join a chat or wade in with an opinion. No wonder many teenagers suffer from what **shrinks** call "decision paralysis". The options are simply too enormous for any human brain to deal with.

30 For many people (not just teenagers), it seems the only way we can validate ourselves is through a screen, a habit which is just as bad for our health as over-indulging in drink or drugs. And just as addictive.

faux: fake, artificial, imitation
shrinks: psychiatrists (doctors that diagnose and treat mental illness)

How do I comment on whole text structure?

To comment on the structure of a text, you need to think about:
- the different elements the writer has selected
- the impact on the reader that the writer intends the elements to have and how they are sequenced.

1 Look at some of the different elements that you might expect to find in an argument text, such as the newspaper article on page 26.

A. ☐ A dramatic and/or attention grabbing opening

B. ☐ Facts and expert opinions

C. ☐ Personal experience

D. ☐ A description and/or explanation of an issue

E. ☐ One or more solutions to that issue

F. ☐ Experiences of people affected by that issue

G. ☐ Encouraging the reader to consider their own experience of that issue

H. ☐ A warning to the reader

I. ☐ A counter argument: an opposing point of view is considered and rejected

a Tick ✓ any of the elements above that you can identify in the text.

b Now label ✐ Text 1 on page 26, to identify where each element you have ticked is used.

2 Think carefully about the impact the writer of the newspaper article intends the structure of the text to have.

a Consider the element the writer places at the beginning of the text. Why do you think the writer decided to begin the article in this way? Write ✐ one or two sentences to explain your ideas.

....

....

b Consider the element the writer places at the end of the text. Why do you think the writer decided to end the article in this way? Write ✐ one or two sentences to explain your ideas.

....

....

c Now look very carefully at the sequence of elements in the rest of Text 1 on page 26. Why do you think the writer decided to sequence these elements in this way? Write ✐ two or three sentences explaining your ideas.

....

....

....

....

....

....

2 How do I identify the impact that sentence structure can have?

The writer's choices of sentence structures can add significant impact to their ideas.

① Which of the following features (a–f) can you identify in the sentences, A–H taken from the newspaper article on page 26? Link ✐ each of the features.

a Questions or exclamations; for example, to encourage the reader to engage with the writer's ideas and/or add emphasis

b Punctuation for effect; for example, to create a dramatic pause and/or add emphasis to an idea

c A long sentence listing items, events or ideas to emphasise their range and impact

d A short sentence to add drama or emphasis to an idea or description

e A balanced sentence of two contrasting clauses

f A sentence in which a key idea or event is delayed until the end of the sentence, to create tension or emphasis

A Do Facebook and Twitter make us happier? ☐

B The answer it would seem is: no. ☐

C But the stress of constantly monitoring our statuses and endlessly documenting every aspect of our lives via networks like Facebook, Snapchat and Instagram is taking its toll. ☐

D It's as if we're starring in a movie of the life we'd like to lead, not the humdrum one we actually inhabit. ☐

E I received 1,000 vile and abusive messages – and they're still coming. ☐

F How many times have we read a message on our phones and then spent hours in turmoil? ☐

G Meanwhile, there have been countless academic studies since 2015 on the negative impacts of social media, showing that its regular use leads to feelings of anxiety, isolation and low self-esteem, not to mention poor sleep. ☐

H And just as addictive. ☐

② ⓐ Read and then choose **two** of the sentences where you feel their structure adds most to the impact of the writer's ideas. Tick ✓ them.

ⓑ Write ✐ a sentence or two about each of your choices, explaining why you chose them.

....

....

....

....

....

....

....

....

....

....

3 How do I comment on the writer's use of structure?

To comment effectively on structure, you should mention at least two, and ideally all, of these key features:

- whole text structure
- sentence structure
- the intended effect of that structural choice
- the impact of that structural choice on the reader.

① Read one student's comment (A–H) on the first two sentences from the article on page 26.

> Do Facebook and Twitter make us happier? The answer it would seem is: no.

A. This rhetorical question engages the reader from the very beginning of the article

B. by encouraging the reader to consider their thoughts and feelings about social media.

C. The writer immediately answers her own question with an emphatic short sentence

D. using a colon to create a dramatic pause.

E. which adds further emphasis to the final word in the sentence: 'no'.

F. This opening question and answer makes clear the writer's argument,

G. which she then develops and justifies in the rest of the article,

H. effectively impressing her point of view on the reader from the start.

Write 🖉 'a', 'b', 'c' or 'd' into each box to show whether you think the phrase comments on the:

a whole text structure

b sentence structure

c intended effect of that structural choice

d impact of that structural choice on the reader.

Put a cross ⊗ if you think the comments don't achieve any of these key features.

② Now write 🖉 two or three sentences to comment on the final sentence of the article:

> And just as addictive.

Aim to comment on the writer's choices of whole text structure and sentence structure, and the effect and impact of this on the reader.

....

....

....

....

....

Commenting on structure

To comment effectively on structure, you need to:

- identify significant elements of whole text structure
- identify significant sentence structures
- comment on their effect
- comment on their impact on the reader.

Now look at the exam-style question you saw at the start of the unit.

Exam-style question

Analyse how the writer uses language and structure to interest and engage readers.

Support your views with detailed reference to the text.

(15 marks)

(**1**) Look at this paragraph from one student's response to the question.

Comments on whole text structure

Comments on sentence structure

> In the middle of the article, the writer moves from general comments on social media to her own experience, highlighting the impact it has had on her personally. Using shorter sentences to add dramatic emphasis to her negative experience, she concludes the paragraph with a final, short blunt sentence detailing the quantity of "vile and abusive messages" she has received. The shocking nature of this incident is heightened still further with punctuation to create a dramatic pause before revealing that these messages are "still coming". The structure of this final sentence is entirely aimed at disturbing the reader and encouraging them to recognise the negative impact that social media can have.

Comments on the effect of these

Comments on their impact on the reader

Can you identify the different features of this student's response? Underline Ⓐ the relevant parts of the paragraph then link 🖉 the annotations to them.

Your turn!

You are now going to write ✏ your own answer in response to the exam-style question, focusing on the writer's use of structure.

Analyse how the writer uses language and structure to interest and engage readers.

Support your views with detailed reference to the text.

(15 marks)

1 Look again at the newspaper article on page 26.

a Note down ✏ two or three key choices the writer has made in structuring the text. You could focus on the beginning, the ending, or the sequence of ideas in the main body of the article.

Key choices writer has made in structuring the text	Effect and impact on the reader

b Add some notes ✏ on the effect and impact on the reader of the writer's choices.

c Look at two or three key sentence structures the writer has used in the article. You could focus on sentence types, sentence length, punctuation or how ideas are ordered within the sentence.

Key sentence structures	Effect and impact on the reader

d Add some notes ✏ on the effect and impact on the reader of the writer's choices.

2 Now write ✏ your response to the exam-style question above on paper.

Review your skills

Check up

Review your response to the exam-style question on page 31. Tick ✓ the column to show how well you think you have done each of the following.

	Not quite ✓	Nearly there ✓	Got it! ✓
commented on whole text structure	☐	☐	☐
commented on sentence structure	☐	☐	☐
developed comments on structure	☐	☐	☐

Look over all of your work in this unit. Note down ✐ the three most important things to remember when commenting on structure.

1. ....

2. ....

3. ....

Need more practice?

Here is another exam-style question, this time relating to Text C on page 75: the newspaper article, 'A Window on Warsaw'. You'll find some suggested points to refer to in the Answers section. ✐

Exam-style question

Analyse how the writer uses language and structure to interest and engage readers.

Support your views with detailed reference to the text.

(15 marks)

How confident do you feel about each of these **skills?** Colour ✐ in the bars.

❶ How do I comment on whole text structure?

❷ How do I identify the impact that sentence structure can have?

❸ How do I comment on the writer's use of structure?

Get started

Explain, comment on and analyse how writers use language and structure to achieve effects and influence readers (AO2)

⑤ Commenting on language and structure

This unit will help you comment on language and structure. The skills you will build are to:

- select evidence that allows you to comment on language and structure
- explore and analyse the combined impact of the writer's use of vocabulary, sentence structures and whole text structures.
- identify and analyse patterns of language and structure.

In the exam, you will face questions like the one below. This is about the text on page 34. At the end of the unit, you will write your own response to this question.

Exam-style question

Analyse how the writer uses language and structure to interest and engage readers.

Support your views with detailed reference to the text.

(15 marks)

The three key questions in the **skills boosts** will help you comment on structure.

 1 How do I choose the right evidence from the text?

 2 How do I build a comment on language and structure?

 3 How do I comment on patterns of language and structure?

Read the extract on page 34 from *Alex's Adventures in Numberland* by Alex Bellos, published in 2010. You will tackle a 21st-century non-fiction extract in the Reading section of your Paper 2 exam.

As you read, remember the following:

Remember the focus of the exam question you are preparing to respond to.	Think about how the writer has selected ideas and structured the text to engage and interest readers.	Think about how the writer's choices of text structure, sentence structure and vocabulary help to add impact to those ideas.

The writer, Alex Bellos, is visiting his friend, Pierre Pica. Pierre has just returned from a trip to the Amazon, where he spent five months living with a community of Indians, the Munduruku.

Text 1 Alex's Adventures in Numberland, Alex Bellos

No one knows for certain, but numbers are probably no more than about 10,000 years old. By this I mean a working system of words and symbols for numbers. One theory is that such a practice emerged together with agriculture and trade, as numbers were an indispensable tool for taking stock and making sure you were not ripped off. The Munduruku are only subsistence farmers and money has only recently begun to circulate in their villages, and so they never evolved counting skills. In the case of the indigenous tribes of Papua New Guinea, it has been argued that the appearance of numbers was triggered by elaborate customs of gift exchange. The Amazon, on the other hand, has no such traditions.

Tens of thousands of years ago, well before the arrival of numbers, our ancestors must have had certain sensibilities about amounts. They would have been able to distinguish one mammoth from two mammoths, and to recognize that one night is different from two nights. The intellectual leap from the concrete idea of two things to the invention of a symbol or word for the abstract idea of "two," however, would have taken many ages to come about. This occurrence, in fact, is as far as some communities in the Amazon have come. There are tribes whose only number words are "one," "two" and "many." The Munduruku, who go all the way up to five, are a relatively sophisticated bunch.

Numbers are so prevalent in our lives that it is hard to imagine how people survive without them. Yet while Pierre Pica stayed with the Munduruku he easily slipped into a numberless existence. He slept in a hammock and he went hunting and ate tapir, armadillo and wild boar. He told the time from the position of the sun. If it rained, he stayed in; if it was sunny, he went out. There was never any need to count.

Still, I thought it odd that numbers larger than five did not crop up at all in Amazonian daily life. I asked Pica how an Indian would say "six fish." For example, just say that he or she was preparing a meal for six people and he wanted to make sure everyone had a fish each.

"It is impossible," he said. "The sentence 'I want fish for six people' does not exist."

What if you asked a Munduruku who had six children: "How many kids do you have?"

Pica gave the same response: "He will say 'I don't know.' It is impossible to express."

However, added Pica, the issue was a cultural one. It was not the case that the Munduruku counted his first child, his second, his third, his fourth, his fifth and then scratched his head because he could go no further. For the Munduruku, the whole idea of counting children was ludicrous. The whole idea, in fact, of counting anything was ludicrous.

Why would a Munduruku adult want to count his children? asked Pica. The children are looked after by all the adults in the community, he said, and no one is counting who belongs to whom. He compared the situation to the French expression *"J'ai une grande famille,"* or "I'm from a big family." "When I say that I have a big family I am telling you that I don't know [how many members it has]. Where does my family stop and where does the others' family begin? I don't know. Nobody ever told me that." Similarly, if you asked an adult Munduruku how many children he is responsible for, there is no correct answer. "He will answer 'I don't know,' which really is the case."

How do I choose the right evidence from the text?

Choosing evidence effectively will enable you to comment on the writer's choices of vocabulary **and** sentence structure **and** whole text structure using just one quotation.

As you read the text, identify quotations that allow you to explore **one** of these features – then think about whether the same quotation would also allow you to comment on **one** or **both** of the others.

① As you read, you might notice a particular sentence structure that adds impact to the writer's ideas. For example:

> He told the time from the position of the sun. If it rained, he stayed in; if it was sunny, he went out. There was never any need to count.

Sentence structure	Vocabulary	Whole text structure
Short simple sentences suggest simplicity of life with the Munduruku		

Add your own notes 🖉 to the table above. Think about:

- how the writer's vocabulary choice adds to the impact of the sentence structures

- how this information, expressed in this way, contributes to the intention and impact of the whole text.

② As you read, you might notice vocabulary choices that add impact to the writer's ideas. For example:

> The Munduruku, who go all the way up to five, are a relatively sophisticated bunch.

Sentence structure	Vocabulary	Whole text structure
	informal language "bunch" creates humour	

Add your own notes 🖉 to the table above. Think about:

- how the structure of this sentence contributes to its impact or effect

- how the writer's use of humour contributes to the impact of the whole text.

2 How do I build a comment on language and structure?

Effective comments often focus on the writer's intention: the impact that the writer intends his texts to have on the reader. You can link and develop your comments on language and structure by exploring how they contribute to the writer's intention.

1 Look at the writer's highlighted vocabulary choices in these sentences.

> For the Munduruku, the whole idea of counting children was ludicrous. The whole idea, in fact, of counting anything was ludicrous.

a How do the writer's vocabulary choices help him to achieve his intention? Annotate 🖉 the quotation above with your ideas.

b How does the writer's choice of sentence structure help him to achieve his intention? Annotate 🖉 the quotation above with your ideas.

c Write 🖉 just **one** sentence commenting on how the writer's choices of both vocabulary and sentence structure help him to achieve his intention.

....

....

....

....

2 Now write 🖉 one or two sentences exploring how the writer's choices in this sentence work together to help him achieve his intention:

> It was not the case that the Munduruku counted his first child, his second, his third, his fourth, his fifth and then scratched his head because he could go no further.

....

....

....

....

....

....

3 How do I comment on patterns of language and structure?

The most sophisticated comments on language and structure identify and explore patterns in the writer's choices: for example, vocabulary choices or sentence structures that create a specific tone in a text.

① Look at the examples of 'types' of vocabulary choice (A–F) below. Then read through the examples of effects or impacts that vocabulary choice can have on the reader (a–i).

A. Emotive vocabulary	a. to create drama
	b. to create sympathy
B. Vocabulary suggesting violence	c. to create a tone of anger or danger
C. Vocabulary suggesting movement	d. to create a sense of energy and sction
	e. to create a colloquial tone
D. Richly descriptive vocabulary	f. to build an intimate, almost friendly relationship with the reader
E. Informal vocabulary	g. to create powerful vivid images
	h. to create humour
F. Formal vocabulary	i. to suggest the writer's expertise

a Which vocabulary type (A–F) can have which effects or impacts (a–i) on the reader? Draw ✐ lines to link them.

b Which of the vocabulary types above are used frequently in the extract on page 34? Tick ✐ them.

c Look at the extract on page 34. Underline Ⓐ and label ✐ three examples of each vocabulary type you have ticked above.

② **a** Which of the following sentence structures are used frequently in the extract on page 34? Tick ✓ them.

- short sentences ☐
- lengthy multiclause sentences ☐
- formal sentence structures ☐
- informal sentence structures ☐

b Underline Ⓐ and label ✐ at least three examples of sentence structure you have identified in the text.

③ Write ✐ one or two sentences commenting on the combined impact of patterns of vocabulary choice and sentence structure in the extract on page 34.

....

....

....

....

Commenting on language and structure

To comment effectively on language and structure, you need to:

- select evidence carefully, thinking about the elements of language and structure you can comment on
- think carefully about the cumulative impact of the writer's choices of whole text structure, sentence structure and vocabulary
- consider patterns of vocabulary and sentence structure choice and their impact on the reader.

Remember: you have only limited time in your exam, so you need to focus on those elements of the text that will allow you to make the most perceptive and developed comments on the writer's choices.

Look at this exam-style question.

Exam-style question

Analyse how the writer uses language and structure to interest and engage readers.

Support your views with detailed reference to the text.

(15 marks)

> The writer occasionally uses informal language to create a humorous, conversational tone, as if he is telling this anecdote directly to the reader. For example, "making sure you were not ripped off." However, in the majority of the extract the writer uses longer, multiclause sentences to suggest his authority and expertise, encouraging the reader to respect the validity of the information he gives.

(1) How would you rate the success of this paragraph? Give each point a score out of 5.

   (a) Selected evidence that will allow comment on language and structure   /5

   (b) Linked comments on language and structure   /5

   (c) Explored patterns of language and structure   /5

(2) How would you improve this paragraph? Write ✏ two or three sentences to suggest ideas the student could add or how their answer could be improved.

....

....

....

....

....

....

Your turn!

You are now going to write ✏️ your own answer in response to the exam-style question.

Exam-style question

Analyse how the writer uses language and structure to interest and engage readers.

Support your views with detailed reference to the text.

(15 marks)

1 What patterns of sentence structure and vocabulary choice have you noticed in the text? Note them down. ✏️

....

....

....

....

....

2 Which of the writer's choices of whole text structure, sentence structure and vocabulary make the most significant contribution to the writer's intention? Note them down. ✏️

....

....

....

....

....

....

....

....

....

....

....

....

3 You should spend around 20–25 minutes on this question, so aim to write ✏️ three or four paragraphs.

    a Which of your ideas noted above will you include in your three or four paragraphs? Tick ✓ them.

    b How will you sequence your ideas? Number ✏️ those that you have ticked.

4 Now write ✏️ your response to the exam-style question above on paper.

Review your skills

Check up

Review your response to the exam-style question on page 39. Tick ✓ the column to show how well you think you have done each of the following.

	Not quite ✓	Nearly there ✓	Got it! ✓
selected quotations that allow me to comment on language and structure	☐	☐	☐
commented on the combined impact of language and structure	☐	☐	☐
explored patterns of vocabulary choice and sentence structure	☐	☐	☐

Look over all of your work in this unit. Note down 🖊 the three most important things to remember when commenting on structure.

1. ....

2. ....

3. ....

Need more practice?

Here is another exam-style question, this time relating to Text A on page 73: an extract from *Nicholas Nickleby* by Charles Dickens. You'll find some suggested points to refer to in the Answers section.

Exam-style question

In lines 10 to 17, how does the writer use language and structure to show the character of Vincent Crummles?

Support your views with reference to the text.

(6 marks)

How confident do you feel about each of these **skills?** Colour 🖊 in the bars.

① How do I choose the right evidence from the text?

② How do I build a comment on language and structure?

③ How do I comment on patterns of language and structure?

⑥ Evaluating texts

This unit will help you evaluate texts. The skills you will build are to:

- identify those features of a text that help the writer to achieve their intention
- develop analysis of a text in order to evaluate its success
- structure an effective evaluation.

In the exam you will face questions like the one below. This is about the text on page 42. At the end of the unit you will write your own response to this question.

Exam-style question

In this extract, there is an attempt to create humour.

Evaluate how successfully this is achieved.

Support your views with detailed reference to the text.

(15 marks)

The three key questions in the **skills boosts** will help you evaluate texts.

 1 What makes a text successful?

 2 Do I analyse or evaluate?

 3 How do I structure an evaluation?

Read the extract on page 42 from *The Canterville Ghost* by Oscar Wilde, a short story first published in 1887. You will tackle a 19th-century fiction extract in the Reading section of your Paper 1 exam.

As you read, remember the following:

Remember the focus of the exam question you are preparing to respond to.	Think about how the writer has tried to create humour.	Think about how the writer's choices of text structure, sentence structure and vocabulary help to achieve that characterisation.

Mr Otis and his wife are wealthy Americans who have decided to move to England. They have bought Canterville Chase, a large mansion that they have been warned is haunted. In this extract, Mr and Mrs Otis arrive at the house.

Text 1 The Canterville Ghost, Oscar Wilde

It was a lovely July evening, and the air was delicate with the scent of the pinewoods. Now and then they heard a wood pigeon brooding over its own sweet voice, or saw, deep in the rustling fern, the burnished breast of the pheasant. Little squirrels peered at them from the beech-trees as they went by, and the rabbits scudded away through the brushwood and over the mossy knolls, with their white tails in the air. As they entered the avenue of

5 Canterville Chase, however, the sky became suddenly overcast with clouds, a curious stillness seemed to hold the atmosphere, a great flight of rooks passed silently over their heads, and, before they reached the house, some big drops of rain had fallen.

Standing on the steps to receive them was an old woman, neatly dressed in black silk, with a white cap and apron. This was Mrs. Umney, the housekeeper, whom Mrs. Otis, at Lady Canterville's earnest request, had consented to

10 keep on in her former position. She made them each a low curtsey as they alighted, and said in a quaint, old-fashioned manner, 'I bid you welcome to Canterville Chase.' Following her, they passed through the fine Tudor hall into the library, a long, low room, panelled in black oak, at the end of which was a large stained-glass window. Here they found tea laid out for them, and, after taking off their wraps, they sat down and began to look round, while Mrs. Umney waited on them.

15 Suddenly Mrs. Otis caught sight of a dull red stain on the floor just by the fireplace and, quite unconscious of what it really signified, said to Mrs. Umney, 'I am afraid something has been spilt there.'

'Yes, madam,' replied the old housekeeper in a low voice, 'blood has been spilt on that spot.'

'How horrid,' cried Mrs. Otis; 'I don't at all care for bloodstains in a sitting-room. It must be removed at once.'

The old woman smiled, and answered in the same low, mysterious voice, 'It is the blood of Lady Eleanore de

20 Canterville, who was murdered on that very spot by her own husband, Sir Simon de Canterville, in 1575. Sir Simon survived her nine years, and disappeared suddenly under very mysterious circumstances. His body has never been discovered, but his guilty spirit still haunts the Chase. The blood-stain has been much admired by tourists and others, and cannot be removed.'

'That is all nonsense,' cried Washington Otis; 'Pinkerton's Champion Stain Remover and Paragon Detergent will

25 clean it up in no time,' and before the terrified housekeeper could interfere he had fallen upon his knees, and was rapidly scouring the floor with a small stick of what looked like a black cosmetic. In a few moments no trace of the blood-stain could be seen.

'I knew Pinkerton would do it,' he exclaimed triumphantly, as he looked round at his admiring family; but no sooner had he said these words than a terrible flash of lightning lit up the sombre room, a fearful peal of thunder

30 made them all start to their feet, and Mrs. Umney fainted.

1 What makes a text successful?

To begin evaluating the success of a text, you need to have a clear overview of what the writer has set out to achieve in their text – and how their ideas support that intention.

1 How would you describe the text type and genre of the text from which the extract on page 42 is taken? Write down 🖉 your ideas, summing them up in 3–5 words.

....

2 Consider what the writer has set out to achieve in each section of the extract.

a What has the writer attempted to achieve in the first paragraph of the extract? Write 🖉 a sentence or two to explain your ideas, including evidence to support them.

....

....

....

b What has the writer attempted to achieve in the middle section of the extract, from lines 8–23? Write 🖉 a sentence or two to explain your ideas, with evidence to support them.

....

....

....

c What has the writer attempted to achieve in the final section of the extract? Write 🖉 a sentence or two to explain your ideas, with evidence to support them.

....

....

....

3 Look at this exam-style question.

Exam-style question

In this extract, there is an attempt to create humour.

Evaluate how successfully this is achieved.

Support your views with detailed reference to the text.

(15 marks)

Now look at all of your answers to question 1. Write 🖉 two or three sentences to sum up how the author attempts to create humour in the extract.

....

....

....

....

....

2 **Do I analyse or evaluate?**

In order to evaluate a text, you first need to make sure you have an overview of the text and how the writer is attempting to achieve their intention. You must then analyse **how** the writer has attempted to achieve their intention **before** you can evaluate the success of the writer's choices.

① You are going to evaluate the writer's success in creating humour in the first paragraph of the text on page 42. One way to tackle an evaluation is to follow these steps:

Identify and analyse the writer's intention

ⓐ Write ✏ a short sentence summing up what the writer has aimed to achieve in the first paragraph.

....

....

....

Evaluate the writer's intention

ⓑ How does this intention contribute to the humour in the extract? Write ✏ a sentence or two to explain your ideas.

....

....

....

Analyse the writer's choices

ⓒ Write ✏ a sentence or two commenting on how the writer's choices in the first paragraph contribute to his intention.

....

....

....

....

Evaluate the writer's choices

ⓓ How successfully do the writer's choices in this section of the text contribute to his attempt to create humour? Write ✏ two or three sentences to explain your ideas.

....

....

....

....

....

....

....

....

3 How do I structure an evaluation?

You can structure an evaluation by working methodically through the text, commenting on each section as you go. However, it is **much** more effective to structure an evaluation **thematically**, focusing on similar ideas or similar effects the writer has achieved or similar techniques the writer has used to achieve them.

① One student noted these thematically related details in the text:

> Typical ghost story
> - overcast weather, rain
>
> - haunted house
>
> - bloodstain
>
> - ....
>
> - ....

What other details might you add to this list? Note 🖉 them above.

② Look at these four details from the text:

A.
> It was a lovely July evening, and the air was delicate with the scent of the pinewoods.

B.
> a great flight of rooks passed silently over their heads

C.
> The old woman smiled, and answered in the same low, mysterious voice, 'It is the blood of Lady Eleanore de Canterville...'

D.
> 'That is all nonsense,' cried Washington Otis...

a How might you connect and comment on the text above? Write 🖉 a sentence or two about each pair.

A + B: ....

....

....

C + D: ....

....

....

b Now think about how all four details work together. Write 🖉 a sentence or two to sum up the cumulative contribution that these four details make to the writer's intention to to create humour.

....

....

....

....

....

....

....

Evaluating texts

A successful evaluation:

- identifies what the writer has set out to achieve
- analyses the choices the writer has made in trying to achieve their intention
- evaluates how effectively the author has achieved their intention
- is structured thematically.

Look at this exam-style question.

Exam-style question

In this extract, there is an attempt to create humour.

Evaluate how successfully this is achieved.

Support your views with detailed reference to the text.

(15 marks)

Then look at a paragraph from one student's response to it.

Identifies the author's intention

Throughout the extract, the writer builds up to the revelation that Mr Otis is totally unconcerned by the legend of the bloodstain, using almost every available stereotype of ghost stories to mislead the reader. Before the legend is revealed, Mrs Otis points out that "something has been spilt", using the vague pronoun 'something' to suggest a shock will come when we learn what the stain is and how it came to be there. Mr Otis, however, bluntly dismisses the legend in a single short sentence: "That is all nonsense." The writer very effectively establishes then completely undermines the stereotypes of the genre, creating humour by misleading then surprising the reader with a sudden change of tone: the nameless terrors of the supernatural need not be feared when they can so easily be removed with Pinkerton's Champion Stain Remover.

Makes a connection between related details/ ideas from the text

Evaluates the writer's success

Analyses the writer's choices

(1) Can you identify the different features of this student's response? Underline Ⓐ or highlight 🖊 the relevant parts of the paragraph then link 🖊 the annotations to them.

Your turn!

You are now going to write your own answer in response to the exam-style question.

Exam-style question

In this extract, there is an attempt to create humour.

Evaluate how successfully this is achieved.

Support your views with detailed reference to the text.

(15 marks)

Before you write your response, complete the tasks below to help you prepare.

(1) What elements of the text will you explore? Read the extract on page 42 again and, as you read, note down ✏ your ideas and any relevant quotations below.

(2) Organise and sequence your ideas in paragraphs. Sort and number ✏ them.

(3) Now write ✏ your response to the exam-style question above on paper. You should spend around 25 minutes on this question and aim to write four or five paragraphs.

Review your skills

Check up

Review your response to the exam-style question on page 47. Tick ✓ the column to show how well you think you have done each of the following.

	Not quite ✓	Nearly there ✓	Got it! ✓
identified what the writer has tried to achieve	☐	☐	☐
analysed how the writer's choices help to achieve their intention	☐	☐	☐
evaluated the writer's success	☐	☐	☐
structured my evaluation thematically	☐	☐	☐

Need more practice?

Here is another exam-style question, this time relating to Text C on page 73: *Nicholas Nickleby* by Charles Dickens. You'll find some suggested points to refer to in the Answers section.

Exam-style question

In this extract there is an attempt to show Nicholas's first experience of the strange and unfamiliar world of actors and acting.

Evaluate how successfully this is achieved.

Support your views with detailed reference to the text.

(15 marks)

How confident do you feel about each of these **skills?** Colour 🖉 in the bars.

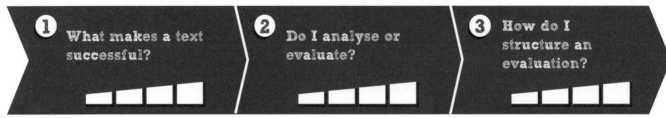

1 What makes a text successful?

2 Do I analyse or evaluate?

3 How do I structure an evaluation?

⑦ Synthesising and comparing

This unit will help you synthesise information and ideas from two texts and compare them. The skills you will build are to:

- identify relevant explicit and implicit information in two texts
- synthesise relevant key ideas and information from two texts
- compare key ideas and information in two texts
- structure your comparison of key ideas and information from two texts.

In the exam you will face questions like the one below. This is about the texts on page 50. At the end of the unit you will write your own response to this question.

Exam-style question

The two texts give information about scientific frauds.

What similarities do the scientific frauds share in these texts?

Use evidence from both texts to support your answer.

(6 marks)

The three key questions in the **skills boosts** will help you synthesise and compare similarities or differences in two texts.

 1 How do I synthesise key points?　　 **2 How do I compare synthesised points?**　　 **3 How do I structure my comparison?**

Read the extracts on page 50, from 'Features of Piltdown Skull "Deliberate Fakes"', an article first published in *The Guardian* newspaper in 1953, and from 'Exploded: the myth of a miracle bomb detector', from Ben Goldacre's *Bad Science* column in *The Guardian* newspaper, published in 2009. You will tackle one 20th-century and one 21st-century non-fiction extract in the Reading section of your Paper 2 exam.

As you read, remember the following:

Remember the focus of the exam question you are preparing to respond to.	Highlight any key information in both texts that is relevant to your response to the exam question.	Consider any similarities or differences in the key information you identify in each text.
☐	☐	☐

In 1912, an amateur archaeologist claimed to have found the skull of a prehistoric ancestor of man near the village of Piltdown in Sussex. The Piltdown skull was revealed to be a fake in 1953.

Text 1 Features of Piltdown Skull "Deliberate Fakes", The Guardian

Recent improvements in the technique of fluorine analysis made possible some of the tests which led three scientists to conclude that the mandible and canine tooth of the "Piltdown skull" were "deliberate fakes." The report of the three investigators – Dr. J. S. Weiner, Dr. K. P. Oakley, and Professor W. E. Le Gros Clark – appears in the Bulletin of the British Museum (Natural History).

5 Fluorine tests carried out in 1949 says the report, did not resolve the seeming contradictions between "a **cranium** closely similar to that of Homo Sapiens" and "a **mandible** and canine tooth of simian form." Not until Dr. Weiner suggested one possible explanation – "the mandible and canine tooth are actually those of a modern ape (chimpanzee or orang) which have been deliberately faked to simulate fossil specimens" – did the investigators take what they now find to be the right track.

10 Experiments produced evidence that the peculiar way in which the teeth were worn down could well have been brought about by the artificial abrasion of chimpanzee's teeth.

Other tests showed that the outer coating on the mandible and teeth did not correspond to that on the cranium. The black coating on the canine tooth turned out to be not, as the first discoverers had thought, ferruginous but "a tough, flexible paint-like substance."

15 "It is now clear (the investigators conclude) that the distinguished palaeontologists and archaeologists who took part in the excavations at Piltdown were the victims of a most elaborate and carefully prepared hoax. The faking of the mandible and canine is so extraordinarily skilful, and the perpetration of the hoax seems to have been so entirely unscrupulous and inexplicable, as to find no parallel in the history of palaeontological discovery."

cranium: the skull
mandible: jaw bone

Four years after this article was published, the founder of ATSC was given a 10-year prison sentence for fraud.

Text 2 'Exploded: the myth of a miracle bomb detector', The Guardian

A British company called ATSC is selling a device which can detect guns, ammunition, bombs, drugs, contraband ivory – and truffles. The ADE651 uses "electrostatic magnetic ion attraction" and can detect these things from a kilometre away, through walls, under the ground, under water or even from an aeroplane three miles overhead.

ATSC's device is handheld. You simply take a piece of plastic-coated cardboard for your chosen target, which
5 has been through "the proprietary process of electrostatic matching of the ionic charge and structure of the substance", pop it into a holder connected to a wand and start detecting.

If there is a bomb on your left, the wand will drift to the left, and point at it. Like a dowsing rod.

Similar devices have been tested repeatedly and shown to perform no better than chance. No police force or security service anywhere in the developed world uses them. But, in 2008, the Iraqi interior ministry bought 800
10 ADE651s for $32m (£19m) and they've ordered a further shipment at $53m. These devices are being used at hundreds of checkpoints in Iraq to look for bombs.

Last week two people working for the New York Times went through nine Iraqi police checkpoints which were using the device, and none found the rifles and ammunition they were carrying (with licences).

Major General Jehad al-Jabiri, of the Iraqi interior ministry, said: "Whether it's magic or scientific, what I care about
15 is it detects bombs."

General Jabiri challenged a New York Times reporter to test the ADE651, placing a grenade and a machine pistol in plain view in his office. Every time a policeman used it, the wand pointed at the explosives. Every time the reporter used the device, it failed to detect anything.

"You need more training," said the general.

1 How do I synthesise key points?

To make an effective comparison, you first need to identify key information, both **explicit** and **implicit**, from each text.

> **explicit:** clearly stated
> **implicit:** implied; not clearly stated

1 Look at these key pieces of information, selected from the first few lines of each text.

Text 1

A.
Recent improvements in the technique of fluorine analysis made possible some of the tests which led three scientists to conclude that the mandible and canine tooth of the "Piltdown skull" were "deliberate fakes."

C.
contradictions between "a cranium closely similar to that of Homo Sapiens" and "a mandible and canine tooth of simian form."

E.
deliberately faked to simulate fossil specimens

Text 2

B.
a device which can detect guns, ammunition, bombs, drugs, contraband ivory – and truffles.

D.
You simply take a piece of plastic-coated cardboard for your chosen target, which has been through "the proprietary process of electrostatic matching of the ionic charge and structure of the substance",

F.
Similar devices have been tested repeatedly and shown to perform no better than chance.

a Label ✎ each one *either*:

- **e** if the information it gives is stated **explicitly** or

- **i** if the information it gives the reader is **implied**.

b Write ✎ one or two sentences to summarise what is implied in the information that you have labelled **i**.

....

....

....

....

....

2 Look again at the key points of information above. Write ✎ two or three sentences summarising any similarities or differences you can identify in the two scientific frauds.

....

....

....

....

....

....

....

3 Now go through both texts on page 50 again, underlining Ⓐ or marking ✎ in the margin any further key points of information in each.

② How do I compare synthesised points?

When you are asked to identify similarities and differences in two texts, you need to synthesise relevant information from both texts. A particularly effective comparison will synthesise a range of linked evidence from different parts of each text.

① Look at one student's comment on the two texts on page 50.

> Both texts provide evidence of fraud, suggesting that neither the Piltdown skull nor the ADE651 was what it appeared to be.

Identify **four** pieces of evidence, two from each text, to support this statement. Underline (A) them in the texts on page 50 and label (✐) them 1A, 1B, 1C and 1D.

② Now look closely at these four pieces of information from the two texts on page 50.

Text 1

...distinguished palaeontologists and archaeologists who took part in the excavations at Piltdown were the victims of a most elaborate and carefully prepared hoax

The faking of the mandible and canine is so extraordinarily skilful... as to find no parallel in the history of palaeontological discovery

Text 2

...in 2008, the Iraqi interior ministry bought 800 ADE651s for $32m (£19m) and they've ordered a further shipment at $53m...

"You need more training," said the general.

a Write (✐) a sentence to explain how you could link the two pieces of information from Text 1.

....

....

....

....

b Now write (✐) a sentence to explain how you could link the two pieces of information from Text 2.

....

....

....

....

c Write (✐) a sentence or two to summarise any similarities or differences between Text 1 and Text 2, using all four pieces of information as evidence.

....

....

....

....

③ How do I structure my comparison?

When you have identified three or four key points of comparison between the texts, you can use them to structure your response.

① Look at the exam-style question on page 49.

a Which of these points of comparison would you use to respond to the question? Tick ✓ them.

		✓	✐
A.	Both texts provide evidence clearly stating or implying fraud.	☐	☐
B.	Both texts use scientific evidence to explain the fraud.	☐	☐
C.	Both texts focus on the victims of the fraud.	☐	☐
D.	Both texts highlight how or why experts have been deceived by the fraud.	☐	☐
E.	Both texts acknowledge the skill with which the fraud was perpetrated.	☐	☐
F.	Text 1 is about a fraud that has been investigated and exposed whereas Text 2 is about a fraud that the writer feels should be investigated and exposed.	☐	☐

b In what order would you sequence your chosen points of comparison? Number ✐ them.

② These sentences are from one paragraph of a student's response to the same question.

		✓	✐
A.	Interestingly, neither text identifies the person or group of people who was responsible for the fraud.	☐	☐
B.	Both texts focus on those who have been deceived by the fraud.	☐	☐
C.	Both texts explain why the frauds' victims have failed to recognise the deception.	☐	☐
D.	Text 1 suggests that the "faking… is so extraordinarily skilful" it is not surprising that the experts did not spot it.	☐	☐
E.	'Text 1 suggests that the "distinguished palaeontologists and archaeologists" who failed to notice the fraud cannot be blamed as the hoax was so "elaborate and carefully prepared".'	☐	☐
F.	Text 2 suggests that the Iraqi Major General should not be blamed for his gullibility as his motives are good: he does not care how the device works, only that "it detects bombs".	☐	☐
G.	Text 2 suggests that Iraqi security forces are convinced the device works: "Every time a policeman used it, the wand pointed at the explosives".	☐	☐

a Which ideas would you include in your response to the exam-style question on page 49? Tick ✓ them.

b How would you sequence the ideas you have chosen? Number ✐ them.

Synthesising and comparing

To synthesise and compare relevant information in two texts, you need to:

- identify relevant key information, both explicit and implicit
- identify and link related information from each text
- organise your comparison effectively.

Note: you do not need to analyse and compare the writers' choices in this type of question. This skill is tested in questions that ask you to compare the writers' viewpoints, perspectives and ideas, which is the focus of Unit 8.

Look at this exam-style question.

Exam-style question

The two texts give information about scientific frauds.

What similarities do the scientific frauds share in these texts?

Use evidence from both texts to support your answer.

(6 marks)

(1) Now look at a paragraph from one student's response to the exam-style question above.

> Both texts highlight the scale of the deception in each scientific fraud. In Text 1, the writer points out that even "distinguished palaeontologists and archaeologists" were deceived by the hoax, describing them as "victims". This is further emphasised in the description of the fraud as "extraordinarily skilful", implying that the fraud's victims were not to blame. The writer of Text 2 uses statistics to show the scale of the fraud, resulting in the Iraqi government spending a total of $75 million on ADE651 devices and, at the time the article was written, with no apparent idea that they were being deceived, making the scale of the fraud all the more shocking, not to mention the danger to thousands of innocent lives caused by using a useless device to detect deadly weapons "at hundreds of checkpoints".

a Which of these key features of a paragraph of effective synthesis and comparison has this student achieved? Tick (✓) them.

i. Links information from each text

ii. Refers to explicit and implied information

iii. Comments on the implications of implied information

iv. Compares information from the two texts

b Annotate (✎) the paragraph above, to show where the student has achieved each key feature you have ticked.

Your turn!

You are now going to write your own answer in response to the exam-style question.

The two texts give information about scientific frauds.

What similarities do the scientific frauds share in these texts?

Use evidence from both texts to support your answer.

(6 marks)

(1) In the space below, note down ✎ at least three different points of comparison you can use in your response.

(2) For each point, note down ✎ two pieces of evidence from each text. Aim to select evidence that supports your point and will allow you to compare the two texts.

(3) For each point, note down ✎ some ways in which you can compare the evidence and the texts.

	Text 1	Text 2	Similar or different? In what ways?
The writer's intention/ideas and attitudes			
Key evidence			
Key choices to explore in that evidence			

(4) Now write ✎ your response to the exam-style question above on paper.

Review your skills

Check up

Review your response to the exam-style question on page 55. Tick ✓ the column to show how well you think you have done each of the following.

	Not quite ✓	Nearly there ✓	Got it! ✓
identified and linked key information from both texts, both explicit and implied	☐	☐	☐
ordered points of comparison effectively	☐	☐	☐
made effective, relevant comparisons	☐	☐	☐

Look over all of your work in this unit. Note down 🖉 the three most important things to remember when synthesising and comparing.

1. ....

2. ....

3. ....

Need more practice?

Here is another exam-style question, this time relating to Text B on page 74, an extract from *English Journey* by J.B. Priestley, and Text C on page 75, *A Window on Warsaw* by Lynda Bailey. You'll find some suggested points to refer to in the Answers section.

Exam-style question

The two texts show the writers' experiences in unfamiliar places.

What similarities and differences are shown in the writers' experiences?

Use evidence from both texts to support your answer.

(6 marks)

How confident do you feel about each of these **skills?** Colour 🖉 in the bars.

① How do I synthesise key points?

② How do I compare synthesised points?

③ How do I structure my comparison?

⑧ Comparing ideas and perspectives

This unit will help you compare the writers' ideas and perspectives in two texts. The skills you will build are to:

- identify key areas for comparison
- compare the writers' ideas, perspectives and intentions
- explore how the writers' ideas, perspectives and intentions are conveyed
- develop an analytical comparison of the writers' choices.

In the exam you will face questions like the one below. This is about the texts on page 58. At the end of the unit you will write your own response to this question.

Exam-style question

Compare how the writers of Text 1 and Text 2 present their ideas and perspectives about animals.

Support your answer with detailed reference to the texts.

(14 marks)

The three key questions in the **skills boosts** will help you compare writers' ideas and perspectives.

1 How do I identify relevant ideas and perspectives?

2 How do I compare ideas and perspectives?

3 How do I develop my comparison?

Read the extracts on page 58 from *All Things Wise and Wonderful* by James Herriot, published in 1977, and *H is for Hawk* by Helen MacDonald, published in 2014. You will tackle two non-fiction extracts, one from the 20th-century and one from the 21st-century, in the Reading section of your Paper 2 exam.

As you read, remember the following:

 The writer's ideas and perspectives in the two texts: how do they describe and respond to animals?

 Any similarities or differences between the two writers' ideas and perspectives.

 Any similarities or differences in the ways the two writers express their ideas and perspectives.

In this autobiographical extract, James Herriot remembers an encounter in his early years as a vet.

Text 1 All Things Wise and Wonderful, James Herriot

There were only six cows in the little cobbled byre with its low roof and wooden partitions and they all had names. You don't find cows with names any more and there aren't any farmers like Mr Dakin, who somehow scratched a living from a herd of six milkers plus a few calves, pigs and hens.

'Aye, well,' he said. 'Ah reckon t'awd lass doesn't owe me anythin'. Ah remember the night she was born, twelve
5   years ago. She was out of awd Daisy and ah carried her out of this very byre on a sack and the snow was comin' down hard. Sin' then ah wouldn't like to count how many thousand gallons o' milk she's turned out – she's still givin' four a day. Naw, she doesn't owe me a thing.'

As if she knew she was the topic of conversation Blossom turned her head and looked at him. She was the classical picture of an ancient bovine; as fleshless as her owner, with jutting pelvic bones, splayed, overgrown feet and
10   horns with a multitude of rings along their curving length. Beneath her, the udder, once high and tight, drooped forlornly almost to the floor.

She resembled her owner, too, in her quiet, patient demeanour. I had infiltrated her teat with a local anaesthetic before stitching but I don't think she would have moved if I hadn't used any. Stitching teats put a vet in the ideal position to be kicked, with his head low down in front of the hind feet, but there was no danger with Blossom. She
15   had never kicked anybody in her life.

Mr Dakin blew out his cheeks. 'Well, there's nowt else for it. She'll have to go. I'll tell Jack Dodson to pick 'er up for the fat-stock market on Thursday. She'll be a bit tough for eatin' but ah reckon she'll make a few steak pies.'

He was trying to joke but he was unable to smile as he looked at the old cow.

Helen Macdonald goes out one morning, hoping to catch a glimpse of a goshawk, a rare bird of prey.

Text 2 H is for Hawk, Helen MacDonald

It was 8.30 exactly. I was looking down at a little sprig of mahonia growing out of the turf, its oxblood leaves like buffed pigskin. I glanced up. And then I saw my goshawks. There they were. A pair, soaring above the canopy in the rapidly warming air. There was a flat, hot hand of sun on the back of my neck, but I smelt ice in my nose, seeing those goshawks soaring. I smelt ice and bracken stems and pine resin. Goshawk cocktail. They were on the
5   soar. Goshawks in the air are a complicated grey colour. Not slate grey, nor pigeon grey. But a kind of raincloud grey, and despite their distance, I could see the big powder-puff of white undertail feathers, fanned out, with the thick, blunt tail behind it, and that superb bend and curve of the secondaries of a soaring goshawk that makes them utterly unlike sparrowhawks. These goshawks weren't fully displaying: there was none of the skydiving I'd read about in books. But they were loving the space between each other, and carving it into all sorts of beautiful
10   concentric chords and distances. A couple of flaps, and the male, the tiercel, would be above the female, and then he'd drift north of her, and then slip down, fast, like a knife-cut, a smooth calligraphic scrawl underneath her, and she'd dip a wing, and then they'd soar up again. They were above a stand of pines, right there. And then they were gone. One minute my pair of goshawks was describing lines from physics textbooks in the sky, and then nothing at all. I don't remember looking down, or away. Perhaps I blinked. Perhaps it was as simple as that. And in that tiny
15   black gap which the brain disguises they'd dived into the wood.

1 How do I identify relevant ideas and perspectives?

Before you can compare two writers' ideas and perspectives, you need to:
- identify each writer's intention – the impact they intend the text to have on the reader
- look very closely at each text, to identify the most significant and/or interesting ideas and perspectives that help the writer to achieve their intention.

① Look again at the two texts on page 58.

a Write ✎ **one** sentence summing up each writer's intention.

Text 1: ....

....

Text 2: ....

....

b Now write ✎ **one** sentence comparing the two writers' intentions. Think about:
- how are they similar
- how are they different?

....

....

....

② **a** Circle Ⓐ **three** key quotes in each of the texts on page 58 that reveal the most interesting or significant ideas and perspectives in each text.

b Look at the quotations you have selected. Note down ✎ at least three words or phrases to describe each writer's ideas and perspectives about animals.

Text 1	Text 2
1	1 ....
....	....
....	....
2	2 ....
....	....
....	....
3	3 ....
....	....
....	....

c Circle Ⓐ and draw ✎ a line linking any **similar** ideas or perspectives in the two texts.

d Underline Ⓐ and draw ✎ a line linking any very **different** ideas or perspectives in the two texts.

2 How do I compare ideas and perspectives?

To write a perceptive comparison of two writers' ideas and attitudes, you need to look closely at **every** choice the writers have made.

(1) You can often find the most significant and interesting ideas and perspectives by reading between the lines.

(a) Look at some of the evidence that one student identified in these two texts. What does each piece of evidence reveal about the writers' ideas and perspectives about the animals they are describing? Annotate (✏) each piece of evidence with your ideas.

Text 1

A.
> Ah remember the night she was born, twelve years ago

B.
> As if she knew she was the topic of conversation Blossom turned her head and looked at him.

Text 2

C.
> I saw my goshawks

D.
> I smelt ice in my nose, seeing those goshawks soaring.

(b) Write (✏) a sentence or two comparing what these four quotations reveal about the writers and their relationships with animals.

....

....

....

....

(2) One way to compare texts is to think about the selection and structure of ideas the writer has used. Look at this summary of each text.

Text 1

- A vet is at a farm where the cows have names.
- He describes the cow he has come to see.
- The farmer decides it must go to slaughter.

Text 2

- The writer goes out one morning and spots a pair of goshawks by chance.
- She describes their flight.
- The goshawks suddenly disappear.

The middle section of each text seems to reveal the most about the writers' ideas and perspectives about animals. However, you need to think about the whole extract.

How do the opening and ending sections of each text add to your understanding of the writers' ideas and perspectives? Write (✏) a sentence or two about each text on page 58.

Text 1: ....

....

Text 2: ....

....

3 How do I develop my comparison?

The most effective comparisons **analyse and compare** the writers' choices and how they contribute to the writer's intention: the impact the writer intends their text to have on the reader.

① What is the writer's intention in each of the texts on page 58? Summarise 🖉 each writer's intention in two or three words.

The writer of Text 1's intention: ....

The writer of Text 2's intention: ....

② Think about how the writer's vocabulary choices in these quotations might contribute to their intention.

Text 1

> as fleshless as her owner, with jutting pelvic bones, splayed, overgrown feet and horns with a multitude of rings along their curving length

Text 2

> he'd drift north of her, and then slip down, fast, like a knife-cut, a smooth calligraphic scrawl, underneath her

Look closely at the similes used to describe the animal. How do these similes help the writer to achieve their intention and convey their ideas and perspectives? Write 🖉 a sentence or two comparing them.

....

....

....

....

....

③ Now look at some of the sentence structures the two writers use.

The writer of **Text 2** uses a lot of shorter sentences:

> And then I saw my goshawks. There they were.

> And then they were gone.

The writer of **Text 1** also uses some shorter sentences.

> She had never kicked anybody in her life.

> Well, there's nowt else for it. She'll have to go.

What do these sentence structure choices contribute to the tone and/or pace of each text? Write 🖉 a sentence or two comparing how the two writers use shorter sentences.

....

....

....

....

....

④ Read the two texts carefully again. Underline Ⓐ and annotate 🖉 any other significant vocabulary or sentence structure choices in each text on page 58, noting their contribution to the writers' intentions.

Comparing ideas and perspectives

To write an effective comparison of two texts, you need to:

- identify each writer's intention, ideas and perspectives
- read each text carefully, looking for significant evidence that explicitly or implicitly reveals each writer's intention, ideas and perspectives
- identify significant points of comparison between the two texts
- explore and compare each writer's choices and their contribution to the writer's intention, ideas and perspectives.

Look again at the exam-style question on page 57.

(1) Now look at the paragraph below, written by a student in response to this exam-style question.

> Both writers suggest a powerful connection between man and the animal kingdom. The writer of Text 1 conveys the emotional bond between farmer and cow very clearly through the details he selects: the farmer names each of his cows (which, the writer points out, does not happen anymore), remembers "the night she was born, twelve years ago", and is obviously upset that "She'll have to go" as he is "unable to smile" while joking about the pies she will be made into. The writer of Text 2 describes a much more active, faster-paced encounter with wild animals: the goshawks "soaring" through and "carving" the sky. However, very much like Text 1, there is a strong suggestion of the personal bond between human and animal in the writer's vocabulary choice, describing them as "my goshawks".

a Annotate (✏) the paragraph, underlining (A) and labelling (✏) to show where in the paragraph this student has:

  i. identified a significant similarity or difference in the writers' ideas and perspectives

  ii. supported their ideas with range of evidence from both texts

  iii. compared how the writers' choices convey their ideas and perspectives and achieve their intention.

b How could this student improve the paragraph above? Write (✏) a sentence or two summarising your ideas.

....

....

....

....

....

....

Your turn!

You are now going to write your own answer in response to the exam-style question.

Exam-style question

Compare how the writers of Text 1 and Text 2 present their ideas and perspectives about animals.

Support your answer with detailed reference to the texts.

(14 marks)

(1) You should spend 20–25 minutes on this kind of question, so should aim to write 🖉 four or five paragraphs. Use the space below to gather and develop your ideas.

	Text 1	Text 2	Similar or different? In what ways?
The writer's ideas and perspectives			
Key evidence			
Key choices to explore in that evidence			

(2) Now write 🖉 your response to the exam-style question above on paper.

Review your skills

Check up

Review your response to the exam-style question on page 63. Tick ✓ the column to show how well you think you have done each of the following.

	Not quite ✓	Nearly there ✓	Got it ✓
identified key areas for comparison	☐	☐	☐
compared the writers' ideas, perspectives and intentions	☐	☐	☐
explored how the writers' ideas, perspectives and intentions are conveyed	☐	☐	☐
developed an analytical comparison of the writers' choices	☐	☐	☐

Need more practice?

Here is another exam-style question, this time relating to Text B on page 74, an extract from *English Journey* by J.B. Priestley, and Text C on page 75, *A Window on Warsaw* by Lynda Bailey. You'll find some suggested points to refer to in the Answers section.

Exam-style question

Compare how the writers of Text B and Text C present their ideas and perspectives about the place they are visiting.

Support your answer with detailed reference to the texts.

(14 marks)

How confident do you feel about each of these **skills?** Colour ✏ in the bars.

1 How do I identify relevant ideas and perspectives?

2 How do I compare ideas and perspectives?

3 How do I develop my comparison?

⑨ Expressing your ideas clearly and precisely

This unit will help you learn how to express your ideas clearly and precisely. The skills you will build are to:

- develop the depth and breadth of your analysis by embedding a range of evidence within it
- choose vocabulary that expresses your ideas precisely
- use a range of sentence structures to express your ideas with clarity.

In the exam you will face questions like the one below. This is about the text on page 66. At the end of the unit you will write your own response to this question.

> **Exam-style question**
>
> In this extract, there is an attempt to show an embarrassing situation.
>
> Evaluate how successfully this is achieved.
>
> Support your views with detailed reference to the text.
>
> (15 marks)

The three key questions in the **skills boosts** will help you express your ideas clearly and precisely.

 1 How do I express my ideas concisely?

 2 How do I express my ideas precisely?

 3 How do I express my ideas clearly?

Read the extract on page 66, from *Vanity Fair* by William Makepeace Thackeray, published in 1848. You will tackle a 19th-century fiction extract in the Reading section of your Paper 1 exam.

As you read, remember the following:

Remember the focus of the exam question you are preparing to respond to ☐

Think about where in the text the writer has tried to show an embarrassing situation. ☐

Think about how the writer's choices of text structure, sentence structure and vocabulary help to achieve their intention. ☐

Amelia Sedley and her fiancée, George Osborne, are enjoying a night out at Vauxhall Gardens in London. Amelia's brother, Jos, is trying to work up the courage to propose to Amelia's best friend, Rebecca Sharp. The two couples have seated themselves in a 'box' and ordered dinner.

Text 1 *Vanity Fair* by William Makepeace Thackeray

The two couples were perfectly happy then in their box: where the most delightful and intimate conversation took place. Jos was in his glory, ordering about the waiters with great majesty. He made the salad; and uncorked the Champagne; and carved the chickens; and ate and drank the greater part of the refreshments on the tables. Finally, he insisted upon having a bowl of rack punch; everybody had rack punch at Vauxhall. "Waiter, rack punch."

5 The young ladies did not drink it; Osborne did not like it; and the consequence was that Jos, that fat **gourmand**, drank up the whole contents of the bowl; and the consequence of his drinking up the whole contents of the bowl was a liveliness which at first was astonishing, and then became almost painful; for he talked and laughed so loud as to bring scores of listeners round the box, much to the confusion of the innocent party within it; and, volunteering to sing a song (which he did in that maudlin high key peculiar to gentlemen in an inebriated state),

10 he almost drew away the audience who were gathered round the musicians in **the gilt scollop-shell**, and received from his hearers a great deal of applause.

"Brayvo, Fat un!" said one; "Angcore!" said another; "What a figure for the tight-rope!" exclaimed another wag, to the inexpressible alarm of the ladies, and the great anger of Mr. Osborne.

"For Heaven's sake, Jos, let us get up and go," cried that gentleman, and the young women rose.

15 "Stop, my dearest diddle-diddle-darling," shouted Jos, now as bold as a lion, and clasping Miss Rebecca round the waist. Rebecca started, but she could not get away her hand. The laughter outside redoubled. Jos continued to drink and to sing; and, winking and waving his glass gracefully to his audience, challenged all or any to come in and take a share of his punch.

Mr. Osborne was just on the point of knocking down a gentleman in top-boots, who proposed to take advantage
20 of this invitation, and a commotion seemed to be inevitable, when by the greatest good luck a gentleman of the name of Dobbin, who had been walking about the gardens, stepped up to the box. "Be off, you fools!" said this gentleman—shouldering off a great number of the crowd, who vanished presently before his **cocked hat** and fierce appearance––and he entered the box in a most agitated state.

"Good Heavens! Dobbin, where have you been?" Osborne said. "Make yourself useful, and take charge of Jos here,
25 whilst I take the ladies to the carriage."

Jos was for rising to interfere—but a single push from Osborne's finger sent him puffing back into his seat again, and the lieutenant was enabled to remove the ladies in safety. Jos kissed his hand to them as they retreated, and hiccupped out "Bless you! Bless you!" Then, seizing Captain Dobbin's hand, and weeping in the most pitiful way, he confided to that gentleman the secret of his loves. He adored that girl who had just gone out; he had broken
30 her heart, he knew he had, by his conduct; he would marry her next morning at St. George's, Hanover Square; he'd knock up the Archbishop of Canterbury at Lambeth: he would, by Jove! and have him in readiness; and, acting on this hint, Captain Dobbin shrewdly induced him to leave the gardens and hasten to **Lambeth Palace**, and, when once out of the gates, easily conveyed Mr. Jos Sedley into a hackney-coach, which deposited him safely at his lodgings.

gourmand: glutton, someone who eats too much
the gilt scollop-shell: the musicians at Vauxhall Gardens performed on a stage in the shape of a scallop shell
cocked hat: a kind of hat worn by army officers in the early 19th century
Lambeth Palace: the official residence of the Archbishop of Canterbury

How do I express my ideas concisely?

Embedding a range of evidence within your comments demonstrates that you can identify significant choices the writer has made. It also allows you to focus your analysis closely on them.

(1) Compare these two comments on the text on page 66.

Student A

> The writer highlights the cause of Jos's embarrassing behaviour at Vauxhall Gardens, describing how "that fat gourmand, drank up the whole contents of the bowl; and the consequence ... was a liveliness which at first was astonishing, and then became almost painful." The phrase "fat gourmand" suggests the writer blames his greed. The words "astonishing" and "painful" suggest how awkward and embarrassing his drunken behaviour was.

Student B

> The writer clearly shows how Jos's embarrassing behaviour develops. Describing him as a "fat gourmand" who "drank up the whole contents of the bowl" clearly suggests the writer blames greed for his "liveliness". At first this "liveliness", euphemistically suggesting drunken behaviour, is simply "astonishing" because it is so out of place and embarrassing, but it soon becomes "painful", suggesting the increasingly agonising discomfort of his humiliated friends.

Which is the most effective, and most effectively expressed, comment? Why?
Write 🖊 a sentence or two to explain your choice.

....

....

....

....

(2) Now look at this comment on Text 1 on page 66.

> Jos's behaviour becomes more embarrassing: "'Stop, my dearest diddle-diddle-darling," shouted Jos, now as bold as a lion, and clasping Miss Rebecca round the waist... The laughter outside redoubled.' The writer shows this by describing his inappropriate behaviour towards Rebecca and the crowd laughing at him.

Rewrite 🖊 the comment above, aiming to embed key elements of the quotation and sharpen the focus of the analysis.

....

....

....

....

....

2 How do I express my ideas precisely?

Sometimes, ideas are best and most clearly expressed using fewer, more carefully chosen words.

1 Look at one student's notes on the presentation of Jos Sedley in the extract on page 66.

| unthinking |
| blundering |
| insensitive |
| inconsiderate |

| eats and drinks too much |
| greedy |
| gluttonous |

Jos

| rude |
| loud |
| badly behaved |
| obnoxious |
| overbearing |

| embarrassing |
| shameful |
| humiliating |

| acts without thinking |
| silly |
| foolish |
| immature |
| impulsive |

a Decide which of the noted words and phrases accurately and appropriately describes how the writer presents the character of Jos. Cross out (X) any words and phrases that are **not** accurate or appropriate.

b Complete the sentence below by choosing the **three** most precise words or phrases to describe how the writer presents the character of Jos.

Jos Sedley is presented as ....

....

....

....

2 Compare these two comments on on the character of Dobbin in the extract on page 66.

Student A

Dobbin is shown to be a brave, kind and helpful person when he frightens away the crowd and saves Jos.

Student B

Captain Dobbin heroically rescues Jos from the crowd.

How has Student B expressed the same ideas in far fewer words? Annotate the responses to explain your ideas.

3 Write **one** sentence commenting on the crowd's response to Jos's behaviour on lines 13–15. Aim to express your ideas as precisely and as concisely as possible.

....

....

....

....

3 How do I express my ideas clearly?

You can use longer, multiclause sentences to link and develop complex ideas. You can also use shorter sentences to summarise, emphasise or clarify your ideas.

① ⓐ Compare these two comments on the extract on page 66. Circle Ⓐ any differences you can spot.

Student A

In the final paragraph of the extract, the writer summarises Jos's romantic intentions using a series of clauses separated by semicolons, suggesting increasingly desperate plans culminating in the intention to "knock up the Archbishop of Canterbury", creating humour by mocking Jos and his embarrassingly misguided plans as the final humiliation of himself and the woman he claims to love.

Student B

In the final paragraph of the extract, the writer summarises Jos's romantic intentions. A series of clauses separated by semicolons suggest increasingly desperate plans culminating in the intention to "knock up the Archbishop of Canterbury", creating humour by mocking Jos and his embarrassingly misguided plans. This is his final humiliation of himself and the woman he claims to love

ⓑ Which version is the most clearly expressed? Write ✏ a sentence or two to explain your choice.

....

....

....

② ⓐ Experiment with restructuring ✏ all the ideas and comments in this very long sentence in two or three shorter sentences.

From the start of the extract, the writer presents Jos as a ridiculous comic figure, describing him as "in his glory" ordering waiters "with great majesty", implying he is conceited and vain, which helps to exaggerate his downfall when he becomes the target of a mocking crowd, which makes him look like a complete fool.

....

....

....

ⓑ Which version is the most clearly expressed: yours or the original version? Write ✏ a sentence or two to explain your choice.

....

....

....

Expressing your ideas clearly and precisely

To express your ideas clearly and precisely, you need to:

- use short embedded quotations, to sharpen your analysis and express it concisely
- choose vocabulary that expresses your ideas precisely
- choose sentence structures that express your ideas clearly.

Now look at the exam-style question you saw at the start of the unit.

Exam-style question

In this extract, there is an attempt to show an embarrassing situation.

Evaluate how successfully this is achieved.

Support your views with detailed reference to the text.

(15 marks)

(1) Look at a short paragraph from one student's response to this question.

> The writer carefully tracks the impact of Jos's drunkenness, taking his friends from happiness to embarrassing carnage. In the opening sentence the couples are "perfectly happy", enjoying "delightful and intimate conversation", suggesting an atmosphere of quiet sophistication. However, within minutes Osborne is "on the point of knocking down a gentleman", Dobbin is "shouldering off a great number of the crowd", Rebecca has "started" but "could not get away", and Jos is "volunteering to sing a song", "puffing" and eventually "weeping". The rapid contrast of happiness collapsing into public humiliation shows how devastating the impact of Jos's foolishness is.

Write ✎ two or three sentences to state what this student has done well and what they could do to improve. Think about:

- their use of embedded evidence
- their choice of vocabulary
- how they have used longer sentences to link ideas
- how they have used shorter sentences for summary, clarity or emphasis.

Your turn!

You are now going to write just **one** paragraph in response to this exam-style question.

Exam-style question

In this extract, there is an attempt to show an embarrassing situation.

Evaluate how successfully this is achieved.

Support your views with detailed reference to the text.

(15 marks)

1 Choose one section of the extract that you will focus on in your paragraph. Write ✐ it in the space below.

2 Underline Ⓐ or circle Ⓐ the writer's choices that you will focus on in your paragraph.

3 Annotate ✐ the choices you have circled or underlined, noting the comments you could include in your paragraph.

4 Write ✐ your paragraph in the space below.

5 Review your writing, asking yourself:

• Can I shorten any longer quotations and embed them more effectively to sharpen my analysis?

• Can I improve any of my vocabulary choices to express my ideas more precisely?

• Can I link any of my ideas more clearly in longer sentences?

• Can I shorten any sentences to summarise, clarify or add emphasis to any of my ideas?

Make any necessary changes ✐ to your paragraph, so that it is as clearly and precisely expressed as possible.

Unit 9 Expressing your ideas clearly and precisely 71

Review your skills

Check up

Review your response to the exam-style question on page 71. Tick ✓ the column to show how well you think you have done each of the following.

	Not quite ✓	Nearly there ✓	Got it! ✓
used embedded quotations to sharpen analysis	☐	☐	☐
selected precise vocabulary	☐	☐	☐
selected sentence structures for clarity	☐	☐	☐

Look over all of your work in this unit. Note down 🖉 the three most important things to remember when reviewing the clarity and precision of your analytical writing.

1. ....

2. ....

3. ....

Need more practice?

You can EITHER:

① Look again at your paragraph written in response to the exam-style question on page 71. Rewrite it 🖉, experimenting with different vocabulary choices and sentence structures, linking your ideas in different ways. Which are most effective in expressing your ideas clearly and precisely?

AND/OR

② Write 🖉 a further paragraph in response to the exam-style question, focusing closely on your use of quotation, vocabulary choice and sentence structures.

How confident do you feel about each of these **skills?** Colour 🖉 in the bars.

① How do I express my ideas concisely?	② How do I express my ideas precisely?	③ How do I express my ideas clearly?
☐☐☐☐	☐☐☐☐	☐☐☐☐

More practice texts

Travelling from London, Nicholas Nickleby stops at an inn for the night. The landlord introduces him to the manager of a travelling theatre company, Mr Vincent Crummles.

Text A Nicholas Nickleby, Charles Dickens

Nicholas was prepared for something odd, but not for something quite so odd as the sight he encountered. At the upper end of the room, were a couple of boys, one of them very tall and the other very short, both dressed as sailors—or at least as theatrical sailors, with belts, buckles, pigtails, and pistols complete—fighting what is called in play-bills a terrific combat, with two of those short broad-swords with basket hilts which are commonly used

5 at our minor theatres. The short boy had gained a great advantage over the tall boy, who was reduced to mortal strait, and both were overlooked by a large heavy man, perched against the corner of a table, who emphatically adjured them to strike a little more fire out of the swords, and they couldn't fail to bring the house down, on the very first night.

'Mr Vincent Crummles,' said the landlord with an air of great deference. 'This is the young gentleman.'

10 Mr Vincent Crummles received Nicholas with an inclination of the head, something between the courtesy of a Roman emperor and the nod of a **pot companion**; and bade the landlord shut the door and begone.

'There's a picture,' said Mr Crummles, motioning Nicholas not to advance and spoil it. 'The little 'un has him; if the big 'un doesn't knock under, in three seconds, he's a dead man. Do that again, boys.'

The two combatants went to work afresh, and chopped away until the swords emitted a shower of sparks: to the
15 great satisfaction of Mr Crummles, who appeared to consider this a very great point indeed.

'That'll be a double ENCORE if you take care, boys,' said Mr Crummles. 'You had better get your wind now and change your clothes.'

Having addressed these words to the combatants, he saluted Nicholas, who then observed that the face of Mr Crummles was quite proportionate in size to his body; that he had a very full under-lip, a hoarse voice, as though
20 he were in the habit of shouting very much, and very short black hair, shaved off nearly to the crown of his head— to admit (as he afterwards learnt) of his more easily wearing character wigs of any shape or pattern.

'What did you think of that, sir?' inquired Mr Crummles.

'Very good, indeed—capital,' answered Nicholas.

'You won't see such boys as those very often, I think,' said Mr Crummles.

25 Nicholas assented—observing that if they were a little better match—

'Match!' cried Mr Crummles.

'I mean if they were a little more of a size,' said Nicholas, explaining himself.

'Size!' repeated Mr Crummles; 'why, it's the essence of the combat that there should be a foot or two between them. How are you to get up the sympathies of the audience in a legitimate manner, if there isn't a little man
30 contending against a big one? —unless there's at least five to one, and we haven't hands enough for that business in our company.'

'I see,' replied Nicholas. 'I beg your pardon. That didn't occur to me, I confess.'

pot companion: a drinking partner, often drunk

In 1933, the writer J.B. Priestley went on a tour of England. In this extract from his book, *English Journey*, he describes Jarrow and Hebburn in the northeast of England. Both towns were suffering from the unemployment and poverty of the Great Depression.

Text B English Journey, J.B. Priestley

The most remarkable giant liner in the world is probably the *Mauretania*, for she is nearly thirty years old and is still one of the fastest vessels afloat. Her record, both for speed and safety, is superb. We are proud of her. Now the *Mauretania* was launched at Wallsend, just across the river from Jarrow; and she has lasted longer than Jarrow. She is still alive and throbbing, but Jarrow is dead.

5   As a real town, a piece of urban civilisation, Jarrow can never have been alive. There is easily more comfort and luxury on one deck of the *Mauretania* than there can ever have been at any time in Jarrow, which even at its best, when everybody was working in it, must obviously have been a mean little conglomeration of narrow monotonous streets of stunted and ugly houses, a barracks cynically put together so that shipbuilding workers could get some food and sleep between shifts. Anything – strange as it may seem – appears to have been good enough for the
10 men who could build ships like the *Mauretania*. But in those days, at least they were working.

Now Jarrow is a derelict town. I had seen nothing like it since the war. My guide-book devotes one short sentence to Jarrow: "A busy town (35,590 inhabitants), has large ironworks and shipbuilding yards." It is time this was amended into "an idle and ruined town (35,590 inhabitants, wondering what is to become of them), had large ironworks and can still show what is left of shipbuilding yards."

15 The Venerable Bede spent part of his life in this neighbourhood. He would be astonished at the progress it has made since his time, when the river ran, a clear stream, through a green valley. There is no escape anywhere in Jarrow from its prevailing misery, for it is entirely a working-class town. One little street may be rather more wretched than another, but to the outsider they all look alike.

One out of every two shops appeared to be permanently closed. Wherever we went there were men hanging
20 about, not scores of them but hundreds and thousands of them. The whole town looked as if it had entered a perpetual penniless bleak Sabbath. The men wore the drawn masks of prisoners of war. A stranger from a distant civilisation, observing the condition of the place and its people, would have arrived at once at the conclusion that Jarrow had deeply offended some celestial emperor of the island and was now being punished. He would never believe us if we told him that in theory this town was as good as any other, and that its inhabitants were
25 not criminals but citizens with votes. The only cheerful sight I saw there was a game of Follow-my-leader that was being played by seven small children. But what leader can the rest of them follow?

After a glimpse of the river-front, that is, of tumble-down sheds, rotting piles, coal dust and mud, we landed in Hebburn, where we pursued, in vain, another man we wanted. Hebburn is another completely working-class town. It is built on the same mean proletarian scale as Jarrow. It appeared to be even poorer than its neighbour. You felt
30 that there was nothing in the whole place worth a five-pound note. It looked as much like an ordinary town of that size as a dust-bin looks like a drawing-room. Here again, idle men – and not unemployable casual labourers but skilled men – hung about the streets, waiting for Doomsday.

This is an article from The Daily Telegraph, published in 2009.

Text C A Window on Warsaw, Lynda Bailey

A friend asked if I would flat-sit for a week. I said, "Of course." She said, "I'm not in Oxford any more. I've moved to Poland."

I look out of her window into the courtyard below. Some weak sunlight struggles over the Palace of Culture to the black-barked tree in the centre. Underneath, a small statue of the Madonna stares through a frill of plastic flowers.
5   Mary and Child seem focused on a set of metal parallel bars. (The courtyard regularly echoes with the thumps of rugs being beaten on these bars. The dust explodes and settles. The flowers are wiped.)

Two drunks are sitting on a concrete planter, their cans of Zywiec beer perched on the pebble-dash trim. The planter is empty, but even with the brightest of bright flowers it wouldn't draw the eye from the grafittied building behind it. This vacant wall is one side of the courtyard and is nine storeys high, windowless, and pitted by Second
10   World War gunfire.

It doesn't worry the huge, black crows. They stomp about eating the lumps of dough brought out by the solid women in the bottom flats. They eat stoically, working their way through the pierogi, the potato, the rye bread. If they were women, they would wear headscarves and thick boots.

A sound of violins and clarinet startles me, but is ignored by the drunks and the birds. It's great music;
15   **Mitteleuropean** music. The sort that makes you feel happy in a sad way. I lean out of the window. Six eyes look up. The music continues. Should I throw some **zlotys** down? Won't even a **grosz** from five floors up be a missile? I dither. They stop. The crows make a big effort to get off the ground.

There's no Shrove Tuesday here and no pancakes. Instead, it's Fat Thursday and doughnuts. Two famous Warsaw cake shops are close to the courtyard. One is a kiosk where a grumpy girl shovels out the cakes without looking at
20   them. The other is a famous patisserie where old women in fur coats sniff around looking for respect. I go to both.

The doughnuts are the best ever. I can see the pale line where they have been turned over in the fat. They are glazed and chewy and full of cherry jam. The dough-fattened crows seek the sun and sit on a thin branch. It bends low, but they ignore it. This is a good day for crows.

There is one grey day. All I see is grey: the concrete, the paving, the planter, the bark of the tree, the sky. Snow
25   drifts down. The crows give up on the dough and shuffle for a place on the patch of grass warmed by the underground pipes. The courtyard becomes white and still. That night I sleep in a muffled world.

It's a courtyard in a city of courtyards, but this one is imprinted on me. I tell my friend I am always available.

mitteleuropean: originating from central Europe
zlotys: the unit of currency in Poland
grosz: a small coin; one hundredth of a zloty

Answers

Unit 1

Page 3

(2) (a) For example:
1. Will Bathsheba agree to marry Oak?
2. Who is telling the truth about Bathsheba's sweethearts – Bathsheba or Mrs Hurst?

(b) For example:
1. The writer creates a contrast between Mrs Hurst's implication that Bathsheba will not wish to marry Oak, with Bathsheba's apparent interest in him.
2. The writer creates a clear conflict between Mrs Hurst's and Bathsheba's accounts of her relationships with men.

Page 4

(1) e.g. At the start of the extract, Oak's proposal seems unlikely to be accepted. However, when Bathsheba runs after him, it suggests he may have some hope. By the end of the extract, when she will not hold his hand, she seems less keen to marry him.

(2) (a) Answers are likely to focus on the outcome of Bathsheba and Oak's relationship.

(b) Mrs Hurst's description of Bathsheba's character, and her ambivalence at the end of the extract, suggest Oak's proposal and Bathsheba's response may have dramatic consequences. Bathsheba running after Oak and her determined denial of other sweethearts suggests a forceful personality, which may exacerbate those dramatic consequences.

(c) The uncertainty and potential drama the writer creates in the extract is intended to engage the reader and manipulate the reader's response to both Oak and Bathsheba.

Page 5

(1) (a) For example:
A: "I'm only an every-day sort of man, and my only chance was in being the first comer."
B: Really and truly I am glad to hear that!"
C: "The lamb isn't really the business I came about, Mrs. Hurst. In short, I was going to ask her if she'd like to be married."

(2) (a) & (b) For example:
A: Bathsheba is manipulative and dishonest. She tells Oak she has no sweethearts (which is not what Mrs Hurst said) and seems to be flirting by encouraging Oak with her hand 'prettily extended upon her bosom' but then rejects his attempt to hold her hand.
B: Bathsheba is wild, unpredictable and unreliable. Mrs Hurst says she is 'wild' and chasing after Oak suggests this too. The way she speaks – emphasising 'SUCH a pity' and her long sentences full of dashes and coordinate clauses – suggests her excitable nature. She is not the right choice for Gabriel Oak.

Page 6

Answer 1 does not fully answer the question. A more explicit suggestion that she may not agree to marry Oak is in her refusal to hold his hand: "she put it behind her, so that it slipped through his fingers like an eel."

Answer 2 is correct and would gain full marks.

Page 7

(1) e.g. "I'm only an every-day sort of man, and my only chance was in being the first comer".

(2) e.g. Bathsheba is "an excellent scholar" but too "wild" to be a governess. She is intelligent but unpredictable.

Page 8

Q	English Journey
	1. From **lines 1–5**, identify **one** reason the writer thinks that the *Mauretania* is 'remarkable'. **(1 mark)**
	2. From **lines 6–17**, give **two** examples that show how Jarrow has changed. **(2 marks)**
A	1. "she is nearly thirty years old and is still one of the fastest vessels afloat."; "Her record, both for speed and safety, is superb."
	2. The men used to have work but are now unemployed; the iron works has closed.

Unit 2

Page 11

(1) For example:
A. The writer and his mother's situation: escaping from a man and hoping to become rich
B. Truck crash
C. Truck crash
E. From the truck crash to the souvenirs
F. The writer exploits his mother's concerns, asking for souvenirs

(2) For example:
A. e.g. short sentences, simple language, little detail
B, C. A dramatic opening, taken out of chronological sequence; vivid, dramatic vocabulary choices
E, F. Contrast of shocked silence following truck crash with the writer's unemotional exploitation; long sentence listing the writer's souvenirs.

Page 12

(1) A. P, A.
B. Q
C. Q
D. Q, A
E. Q, A

(2) **a** All are valid responses.

b e.g. A, B, C, E, D

c e.g. (based on the suggested response to 2b: P, A, A, Q, Q, Q, A, Q, A): The key point here is to recognise that, while paragraphs of analysis should feature a point, some evidence and some analysis or explanation, the most effective paragraphs of analysis do not follow a rigid and restrictive structure.

Page 13

(1) For example:

a Positioning the sentence at the end of the paragraph, following the writer's earnest attempts to stop himself asking for souvenirs, sets it as a kind of punchline to the story, creating humour.

b The listing of the souvenirs emphasises their quantity.

c The writer emphasises the detail of the souvenirs, e.g. "beaded… brass… tooled-leather…", suggesting their expense and the pleasure he takes in them.

d All the above choices are intended to create humour, and to suggest a ruthless side to the writer's character.

e The contrast of the truck crash and the writer's ruthless exploitation adds to the humour and our understanding of his character.

Page 14

(1) For example:

* the lack of detail also suggests the naïve simplicity of the plan: "to get rich"

* the brevity of the paragraph adds to the emphatic simplicity of the plan

* his mother was "afraid of" the man they are running from, implying a violent and dangerous relationship.

Page 16

Q	Nicholas Nickleby
	In the first paragraph, how does the writer use language and structure to create a humorous description of the scene?
	Support your views with reference to the text.
	(6 marks)
A	**Language**
	• The narrator describes "something odd"
	• Humorous listing of the actors' costumes: "belts, buckles, pigtails, and pistols"
	Structure
	• Exaggerated contrast of the two actors: "one of them very tall and the other very short"
	• Lengthy sentence that contrasts the battling actors and the "heavy man", concluding with his certainty that they will "bring the house down, on the very first night"

Unit 3

Page 19

(1) All are arguable.

(2)–**(4)**. For example:

A, F: sorrow is denied then acknowledged at the breaking of the doll, suggesting the power of communication to bring emotional awareness.

B, C, E: "the still dark world" of the writer is contrasted with "the warm sunshine" of the outside world and the vibrancy of objects that "quiver with life" once the writer has made her breakthrough in communication.

A, D, E: The writer's positive response to the destruction of her doll is transformed into the "light, hope, joy" of her discovery and contrasted with her "repentance and sorrow".

Page 20

(1) e.g. "Living" suggests that the word has brought life to the water and to the world in which the writer lives – and that the word has gained life through the writer's understanding of the connection between the world and language.

e.g. "Awakened" suggests the life the word has brought – and that the writer was unconscious of the world before she made the connection between language and the world it describes.

(2) **a** e.g. The writer describes her childish pleasure in breaking the doll, without "sorrow or regret". The writer exaggerates the impact in emphasising how she is "keenly delighted" by the violence of "seizing the doll" which she then "dashed… upon the floor."

b e.g. The writer draws attention to the cause of her frustration in describing "the still, dark world in which I lived".

c e.g. In emphasising her disability and her anger, the writer effectively suggests her frustration and so prepares the reader to respond empathetically to the triumphant realisation she reaches at the end of the extract.

Page 21

(1) **a** **b** & **c** For example:

B: "That living word awakened my soul, gave it <u>light, hope, joy, set it free!</u>"

D: "Everything had a name, and each name <u>gave birth</u> to a new thought. As we returned to the house every object which I touched seemed to <u>quiver</u> with life."

E: "<u>seizing</u> the new doll, I <u>dashed</u> it upon the floor"

c & **d** e.g. The writer creates a tone of astonishment and surprise in describing her realisation that language describes the world and creates thought. In describing this as a "birth", the writer suggests the life that language creates and her astonishment at it, while the word "quiver" suggests the power and vibrancy that language brings to her world.

Page 22

Identifies a pattern of language use	"pleasure and pride" ... However, this pleasure is echoed in much less positive circumstances when she is "keenly delighted" by smashing her doll.
Comments on tone	A tone of violence and anger in the writer's frustration is created through her language choice: the child "seized" the doll and "dashed it upon the floor".
Focuses on the impact of the writer's language choices on the reader	In highlighting the success and failure of her lessons, the writer seems to be offering the reader two possible responses to her younger self: sympathy for her struggle and a more negative response to her anger.
Explores a range of meanings and/or responses	However, for some readers the strongest response might be sympathy for the writer's long-suffering teacher.

Page 24

Q	English Journey
	Analyse how the writer uses language and structure to interest and engage readers.
	Support your views with detailed reference to the text.
	(15 marks)
A	Language
	• Consistently negative: "derelict... stunted... ugly".
	• Contrast with the *Mauretania's* "comfort and luxury"
	• Emphasises the impact on the people of Jarrow: "hundreds and thousands of them... the whole town..."
	Structure
	• Frequent use of short sentences to emphasise blunt conclusions: "Now Jarrow is a derelict town."
	• Contrast of the *Mauretania* and the town that built it: "She is still alive and throbbing, but Jarrow is dead."
	• Comparison of Hebburn to Jarrow, suggesting it is even more run down.

Unit 4

Page 27

① ⓐ A, B, C, D, E, F, G, H

② ⓐ e.g. The writer begins with some surprising, shocking facts about social media to gain the reader's attention and interest.

   ⓑ e.g. The writer ends with a disturbing warning, reinforcing the dangers of social media by comparing its use to an alcohol or drug addiction.

   ⓒ e.g. The writer progresses from the general to the personal: she establishes the problem before reinforcing its impact through her own personal experience then finally inviting the reader to consider their own personal experiences of social media.

Page 28

① & ②

A: a short, rhetorical question engages the reader, inviting consideration

B: a short sentence in which punctuation is used to create a dramatic pause before an emphatic denial.

C: a sentence listing the various demands and networks of social media with a dramatic ending to emphasise the problems of social media.

D: a balanced sentence contrasts image and reality to highlight the pressures of social media

E: a short sentence in which punctuation is used to create a pause before a disturbing conclusion.

F: a rhetorical question invites the reader to acknowledge their own experience of the pressures of social media

G: a long sentence listing the impact of social media on people's well-being

H: a short sentence adds emphasis to this final, disturbing point

Page 29

① A. a, b, c
  B. d
  C. b
  D. b, c
  E. c
  F. a, b, c
  G. a
  H. d

② e.g. This is an emphatic short sentence positioned at the very end of the article, to provide a shocking and disturbing summary of the great dangers of social media for the reader.

Page 30

Comments on whole text structure	In the middle of the article, the writer moves from general comments on social media to her own experience, highlighting the impact it has had on her personally.
Comments on sentence structure	The writer concludes the paragraph with a final, short blunt sentence detailing the quantity of "vile and abusive messages" she has received.
Comments on the effect of these	The writer uses shorter sentences to add dramatic emphasis to her negative experience. The shocking nature of this incident is heightened still further with punctuation to create a dramatic pause, before revealing that these messages are "still coming".
Comments on their impact on the reader	The structure of this final sentence is entirely aimed at disturbing the reader and encouraging him/her to recognise the negative impact that social media can have.

Page 32

Q	A Window on Warsaw
	Analyse how the writer uses language and structure to interest and engage readers.
	Support your views with detailed reference to the text. (15 marks)
A	**Language**
	• Descriptive language builds vivid, evocative images: "weak sunlight struggles"; "glazed and chewy and full of cherry jam"; "a muffled world".
	• The writer creates humorous images "The dust explodes and settles. The flowers are wiped"; "If they were women, they would wear headscarves and thick boots."
	Structure
	• Very short first paragraph reflects the shock of being asked to flat-sit in Poland.
	• Frequent short sentences suggest flitting thoughts and revealing snapshots of Warsaw life.
	• The progression from urban decay, to the humour of the crows, to the pleasures of music and doughnuts suggests the writer's growing pleasure.

Unit 5

Page 35

1. e.g. Simple vocabulary reflects simplicity of sentence structure; this section of the text supports the writer's intention of explaining the lives of a people to whom numbers are largely irrelevant; the writer's choices suggest an appealing simplicity, rather than lack of sophistication or intelligence.

2. e.g. The writer positions the noun phrase "relatively sophisticated bunch" at the end of the sentence to add emphasis to the humorous vocabulary choice (compare, for example, a less concise and less carefully crafted version of the sentence: "The Munduruku are a relatively sophisticated bunch because they go all the way up to five.") Humour helps the writer engage and entertain readers as the author highlights the concept of numbers and counting and their relative importance to different cultures.

Page 36

1. a) e.g. The writer uses repetition of sentence structure and vocabulary, notably of the forceful adjective "ludicrous", to emphasise how insignificant numbers are to the Munduruku.

2. e.g. The writer creates humour by structuring the sentence to suggest an imaginary Munduruku counting his children and then completing the vivid comic image with the informal phrase "scratched his head". This image effectively mocks the "ludicrous" idea that the Munduruku need to count their children – or anything else.

Page 37

1. a) e.g. A: a, b.
   B: c
   C: d
   D: g
   E: e, f, h
   F: i

b) & c) Largely formal vocabulary choices dominate, with occasional informal vocabulary choices, for example "indispensable... sensibilities... occurrence...", "ripped off... bunch... kids"

2. Formal, lengthy multiclause sentences dominate as the writer explains complex ideas and maintains a tone of expertise and authority.

Some informal, shorter sentences create an intimate tone, suggesting conversation with the reader; for example, "By this I mean a working system of words and symbols for numbers."

3. e.g. The combination of largely formal sentence structures and vocabulary choices, with occasional, colloquial informality, creates a tone of authority but an intimate, friendly relationship between the writer and reader.

Page 40

Q	Nicholas Nickleby
	In lines 10 to 17, how does the writer use language and structure to show the character of Vincent Crummles?
	Support your views with reference to the text. (6 marks)
A	**Language**
	• His "great satisfaction" at the drama suggests his pride in his work.
	• "Get your wind" suggests his kindness and considerateness.
	Structure
	• Contrasting description suggests self-importance ("the courtesy of a Roman emperor") and friendliness ("the nod of a pot companion").
	• Short clauses in dialogue suggest rapid thought and impatience: "There's a picture.... Do that again, boys."

Unit 6

Page 43

1. A comic ghost story

2. a) e.g. The writer creates a hyperbolically perfect rural scene before a stereotypically ghostly storm destroys the peace.

   b) e.g. The mockery of the ghost genre continues in every element of the middle section: the haunted house, the elderly servant, the blood stain, the ancient legend, etc.

   c) e.g. The writer mocks the genre further in the response of the Americans: they dispel the stain and the legend with a simple cleaning product.

3. e.g. The writer effectively creates humour through selecting exaggeratedly stereotypical elements of the ghost genre that have no effect on those characters who, traditionally, should be the victims of the story.

Page 44

1. a) A perfect rural scene is disturbed by an ominous storm, typical of ghost stories.

(b) The writer is mocking the ghost story genre through hyperbole and stereotype.

c / d For example: positive adjectives, "lovely… delicate… sweet" and an array of small, appealing animals suggesting a rural idyll are contrasted with ominous "rooks" passing "silently" and a suddenly "overcast" sky.

The writer humorously contrasts a hyperbolically perfect summer evening with a stereotypically ghostly storm, effectively mocking the ghost story tradition.

Page 45

(1) For example: rooks, old housekeeper, haunted house, legend of murder, lightning

(2) (a) In A and B the writer uses contrast to exaggerate the ghostly disturbance of a rural idyll.

In C + D the writer uses contrast to emphasise the difference between believer and non-believer.

(b) Having established the genre stereotypes of A, B and C, the response of Mr Otis is all the more surprising and humorous.

Page 46

Identifies the author's intention	Throughout the extract, the writer builds up to the revelation that Mr Otis is totally unconcerned by the legend of the bloodstain, using almost every available stereotype of ghost stories to mislead the reader.
Makes a connection between related details/ideas from the text	Before the legend is revealed, Mrs Otis points out that "something has been spilt", using the vague pronoun 'something' to suggest a shock will come when we learn what the stain is and how it came to be there.
Analyses the writer's choices	Mr Otis, however, bluntly dismisses the legend in a single short sentence: "That is all nonsense."
Evaluates the writer's success	The writer very effectively establishes then completely undermines the stereotypes of the genre, creating humour by misleading then surprising the reader with a sudden change of tone: the nameless terrors of the supernatural need not be feared when they can so easily be removed with Pinkerton's Champion Stain Remover.

Page 48

Q	*Nicholas Nickleby*
	In this extract there is an attempt to show Nicholas's first experience of the strange and unfamiliar world of actors and acting.
	Evaluate how successfully this is achieved.
	Support your views with detailed reference to the text.
	(15 marks)

A	• The writer introduces the strange scene as "something odd" and focuses on a scene seemingly chosen for its oddness!
	• Crummles keeps Nicholas away from the scene suggesting his lack of understanding: "not to advance and spoil it".
	• Nicholas does not understand that an unfair fight is more dramatic.

Unit 7

Page 51

(1) (a) & (b) B, D and F imply that the device is fraudulent. B implies this in the range and nature of those items it is claimed it can detect; D contrasts its cardboard construction with the manufacturer's spurious scientific claims; F strongly suggests the device is worthless.

(2) Both articles identify fraudulent claims, although Text 2 only implies deception while Text 1 states it explicitly. Both use scientific terminology to describe the two objects, however Text 1 uses the terminology to describe the process through which the fraud was discovered, while Text 2 implies that the terminology the manufacturer uses to describe the object is fraudulent.

(3) Selections of key information are likely to focus on:

- Text 1: details of how the skull was created; the investigators' conclusions on the scale of the hoax and the motives of its perpetrators.
- Text 2: the faith which some have placed in the device; the money they have spent on the device; those who have sought to discredit the device.

Page 52

(1) For example:

- Text 1: artificial abrasion of chimpanzee's teeth… The black coating on the canine tooth turned out to be … "a tough, flexible paint-like substance."
- Text 2: two people working for *The New York Times* went through nine Iraqi police checkpoints that were using the device, and none found the rifles and ammunition they were carrying… Every time the reporter used the device, it failed to detect anything.

(2) (a) For example: The article highlights how "skilful" the fraud was, fooling even "distinguished" experts.

(b) The article highlights how entirely the Iraqi government rely on the device to detect arms.

(c) Both articles highlight the victims of the fraud and how deeply they were deceived.

Page 53

(1) B is not a valid point of comparison. Text 1 uses scientific evidence to explain the fraud. Text 2 uses spurious scientific claims made by the manufacturers of the device in order to discredit it.

C is a valid point of comparison, although the point is expressed more perceptively in D.

F is a valid point of comparison but refers to a difference rather than a similarity.

A and E are valid points of comparison relevant to the exam-style question.

② **ⓐ** All the ideas are valid.

ⓑ For example: B, E, F, C, D, G, A.

Page 54

A. Links information from each text	"distinguished palaeontologists and archaeologists" were deceived by the hoax, describing them as "victims". This is further emphasised in the description of the fraud as "extraordinarily skilful". The writer of Text 2 uses statistics to show the scale of the fraud... $75 million... "at hundreds of checkpoints"
B. Refers to explicit and implied information	"distinguished palaeontologists and archaeologists" were deceived by the hoax, describing them as "victims". This is further emphasised in the description of the fraud as "extraordinarily skilful". The writer of Text 2 uses statistics to show the scale of the fraud... $75 million... "at hundreds of checkpoints".
C. Comments on the implications of implied information	implying that the fraud's victims were not to blame the danger to thousands of innocent lives
D. Compares information from the two texts	Both texts highlight the scale of the deception in each scientific fraud.

Page 56

Q	*English Journey,*and *A Window on Warsaw* The two texts show the writers' experiences in unfamiliar places. What similarities and differences are shown in the writers' experiences? Use evidence from both texts to support your answer. **(6 marks)**
A	• Both texts describe decay. Text 1 "Jarrow is a derelict town"; Text 2: "graffitied building... pitted by Second World War gunfire." • Both texts describe people in difficult situations. Text 1: "The men wore the drawn masks of prisoners of war." Text 2: "Two drunks are sitting on a concrete planter". • Both texts describe positive experiences, although only one in Text 1: "The only cheerful sight I saw there was a game of Follow-my-leader"; Text 2:" A sound of violins and clarinet startles me, but is ignored by the drunks and the birds. It's great music..."

Unit 8

Page 59

① **ⓐ** For example:
- Text 1: the writer conveys the powerful bond between a farmer and his cow.
- Text 2: the writer admires the beauty and agility of a pair of goshawks.

ⓑ Both writers aim to convey the relationship between human and animal, although one conveys an emotional bond while the other conveys a sense of amazement and admiration.

② **ⓑ** For example:
- Text 1: emotional, emotive, sympathetic
- Text 2: admiring, emotional, dramatic.

Page 60

① **ⓑ** While Text 1 suggests a powerful emotional relationship between human and animal, Text 2 focuses on the dramatic impact that wild animals can have on humans.

② Text 1: the opening and ending frame the description of the patient, pitiful cow in the context of the farmer's treatment of, and attitude to, the life and death of his animals.

Text 2: the opening suggests how lucky the writer is to enjoy this chance encounter; the ending reinforces this, and the birds' almost supernatural speed and agility.

Page 61

① For example:
- Text 1: affectionate bond
- Text 2: admiration and drama.

② The simile in Text 1 highlights the similarities of the farmer and his cow, further suggesting their bond. The simile in Text 2 suggests the precision, agility and drama of the birds in flight.

③ While the writer of Text 1 uses short sentences to add emphasis to the emotional and dramatic decision to slaughter the cow, the writer of Text 2 uses short sentences to suggest the pace and drama of the goshawks' flight.

④ For example:

Lengthy, descriptive listing of carefully selected, indicative features:

Text 1:
- jutting pelvic bones, splayed, overgrown feet and horns

Text 2:
- the big powder-puff of white undertail feathers, fanned out, with the thick, blunt tail behind it, and that superb bend and curve of the secondaries

Telling visual details of appearance/behaviour of the animals:

Text 1:
- Beneath her, the udder, once high and tight, drooped forlornly almost to the floor.
- her quiet, patient demeanour

Text 2:
- Goshawks in the air are a complicated grey colour... a kind of raincloud grey
- he'd drift north of her, and then slip down, fast, like a knife-cut, a smooth calligraphic scrawl underneath her, and she'd dip a wing, and then they'd soar up again.

Page 62

(1) (a) For example:

A. identified a significant similarity or difference in the writers' ideas and perspectives	Both writers suggest a powerful connection between man and the animal kingdom.
B. supported their ideas with range of evidence from both texts	the farmer names each of his cows (which, the writer points out, does not happen anymore), remembers "the night she was born, twelve years ago", and is obviously upset that "She'll have to go" as he is "unable to smile" while joking about the pies she will be made into.... the goshawks "soaring" through and "carving" the sky.
C. compared how the writers' choices convey their ideas and perspectives and achieve their intention.	The writer of Text 2 describes a much more active, faster-paced encounter with wild animals... However, very much like Text 1, there is a strong suggestion of the personal bond between human and animal in the writer's vocabulary choice, describing them as "my goshawks".

(b) This response could be strengthened with more analysis of the writer's choices in Text 1.

Page 64

Q	**English Journey** and **A Window on Warsaw** Compare how the writers of Text 1 and Text 2 present their ideas and perspectives about the place they are visiting. Support your answer with detailed reference to the texts. (14 marks)
A	• Both writers are focus on negative elements of urban life. Text 1: "narrow, monotonous... stunted... ugly... derelict". Text 2: Text 2: "plastic flowers... concrete planter... metal parallel bars". • Text 2 uses humour: "If they were women, they would wear headscarves and thick boots." Text 1 is relentlessly negative, focusing on the poverty of Jarrow and Hebburn's inhabitants. • Text 2 highlights several positive elements: "It's great music... The doughnuts are the best ever." and, despite the predominance of urban grey, she is keen to return: "I am always available".

Unit 9

Page 67

(1) Student B's comment is the most effective, using short embedded quotations to allow closely focused analysis of each of the writer's significant choices.

(2) For example: Jos's embarrassing drunkenness makes him "as bold as a lion". Calling Rebecca "my dearest diddle-diddle-darling" suggests that he has lost all his inhibitions, allowing him to use embarrassingly sentimental language and embarrassingly physical contact, "clasping Miss Rebecca round the waist". The crowd's "laughter" is "redoubled", emphasising that Jos is not just embarrassing himself but humiliating his friends in front of an audience.

Page 68

(1) (b) All are arguable, however 'foolish', 'shameful' and 'inconsiderate' are perhaps the most precise.

(2) Student B has condensed the string of adjectives 'brave, kind and helpful' in the adverb 'heroically' and the verbs 'frightens away' and 'saves' in the verb 'rescues'.

Page 69

(1) (b) Student B's response is more clearly expressed. Student A's links too many ideas in a very long sentence. Student B expresses the same ideas, summarising her key point in the short opening sentence, linking two points of analysis in her longer second sentence, and summarising her analysis of its impact in the final, short sentence.

(2) (a) For example: From the start of the extract, the writer presents Jos as a ridiculous comic figure. He is described "in his glory" ordering waiters "with great majesty", implying he is conceited and vain, which helps to exaggerate his downfall when he becomes the target of a mocking crowd. Throughout the extract he is made to look like a complete fool.

Page 70

The student has:
- very effectively selected and linked a range of evidence from the entire text
- selected precise vocabulary
- used shorter sentences to make a clear point at the beginning of the paragraph and summarise their analysis at the end.

The student could have:
- incorporated more close analysis of key choices in some quotations, however this might have resulted in an extremely long, unwieldy sentence, weakening the focus of the analysis of pace and contrast.